MENTAL TOUGHNESS
FOR YOUNG ATHLETES

THE BLUEPRINT ON HOW TO PUSH PAST FAILURE, REMAIN COMPETITIVE, AND BRING YOUR A-GAME ON THE FIELD

PAUL HARDY

IPPOCERONTE
publishing

CONTENTS

INTRODUCTION

Have you ever wondered what it would be like to be a professional athlete? Besides eating a healthy diet and getting to bed before midnight, what else comes with being a high-performing sportsman or woman?

The fame that follows athletes often distracts us from the real sacrifices they make on their journey to the top. For instance, we might celebrate a football player signing a million-dollar endorsement deal but overlook the many hours of training and personal development they had to endure to be chosen for that kind of opportunity.

Therefore, for the purpose of this book, we will explore the less glamorous side of being an athlete—the side that hardly anyone speaks about. We will look at inspirational stories of the world's most talented sports players and learn lessons from how they were able to overcome obstacles.

The truth is that tough times are what test the character of an athlete. For example, getting an injury, being rejected by a team, or being told that you are not good enough are some of the things that test the strength of an athlete's character.

What makes a strong character?

If I were to describe a strong character in one word, it would be resilient. The word resilience comes from the Latin word resilire, which means "to jump back." An athlete with a strong character has the ability to bounce back from setbacks and make a quick recovery. They don't quit after the first, second, or third failure; instead, they look at failure as valuable feedback to use when adjusting their approach toward their goals.

Athletes with strong character are immune to the word 'No' and won't allow any kind of challenge to get in the way of achieving their goals. There are no limits to how far they can push their bodies and stretch their minds. To say they are resilient is quite frankly an understatement.

As a young athlete, you aspire to develop your talent and become a professional athlete one day, but to manifest your dreams you will need to apply more than just hard work. This book will teach you about the concept of mental toughness and how it can help you improve your approach toward your sporting career.

Mental toughness is the ability to stay committed to your goals despite the hardship you may endure along your journey. It gives you what I call the "staying power" so you are able to follow through with your goals until you eventually achieve them. As an athlete, mental toughness can shift your mindset from scarcity to abundance. It can boost the confidence you have in yourself to succeed and keep up with the demands of your lifestyle and training. But best of all, mental toughness can help you build a strong character so you can be courageous in the face of opposition.

No one is born mentally tough, but anyone who is willing to get out of their comfort zone and believes in their potential can certainly master this skill. Are you that person?

CHAPTER 1

THE COST OF BEING A HIGH-PERFORMING ATHLETE

I feel [an] endless need to learn, to improve, to evolve, not only to please the coach and the fans, but also to feel satisfied with myself.
— Cristiano Ronaldo

A COMMITMENT TO EXCELLENCE

Cristiano Ronaldo, famously nicknamed CR7, is a living football legend. At the age of 36, the Portuguese national has already received five FIFA Ballon d'Or awards—the most achieved by any European player—and he also holds the record for the most goals scored in the UEFA Champions League.

What is Ronaldo's secret weapon that has made him one of the best sportsmen of our time?

For starters, it isn't talent. It may come as a shock that Cristiano Ronaldo was never the strongest footballer on the field. When he began his career, he didn't display as much talent as other young footballers at the time. Nevertheless, he made up for his lack of talent by being the most hard-working athlete on his team.

Ronaldo's work ethic has been studied and written about a number of times over the course of his career. His desire to be the best footballer of all time meant that he would need to work harder than many of the footballers he admired, like David Beckham and Lionel Messi.

He focused on being one step ahead of his teammates in everything they did. For example, during training sessions, Ronaldo developed a habit of starting his drills an hour before his teammates arrived, and continued practicing even after the training session had ended.

He also went the extra length of improving his physical fitness by increasing the intensity of his workouts. As a young player, he would put ankle weights on his feet to make his training more difficult. Training with heavy weights improved his footwork during real matches and made him stronger and faster!

Some might think Ronaldo was born with supernatural strength, but his power was developed through his commitment to excellence. He set the bar high for himself and refused to lower it even when his expectations seemed unreasonable to many. In his own words:

"We fight to be the best and this is why this is my main point, it's my motivation – it's to be better than them. That's not just now or in the future, but this year, next year, every year"
(RSNG Team, 2020).

TALENT DOESN'T GUARANTEE SUCCESS

What is the cost of being a high-performing athlete? I can summarize it in two words—hard work.

Hard work is what keeps the momentum going when seeking to achieve goals. It keeps you focused and capable of constantly making progress, regardless of how small or big your progress may be. Hard work requires you to exert physical energy. This means that the amount of action you are willing to take measures the amount of effort you put into your work.

Let's continue to use Cristiano Ronaldo's football career as an example to illustrate the importance of hard work. Going into his career, Ronaldo knew that he wanted to become one of the greatest football players of all time. As ambitious as his goal was, he was committed to putting in the work required to achieve it. This meant that he needed to work harder than any other player on his team, or in his league, in order to get ahead. Ronaldo's competitive spirit helped him develop an extraordinary work ethic, which eventually ended up being more valuable than his talent.

If getting to the top requires hard work, where does talent fit in?

Talent is the natural skill or ability that someone is born with. An athlete who is talented at their sport doesn't require a lot of practice to show an advanced level of skill. Their inherited trait or gift causes them to perform like a pro without even trying.

Being talented in a sport is a valuable quality to have because it gives you a competitive edge. The kind of skill that takes other athletes years to master comes naturally to you. Talented athletes are usually those who end up breaking world records or using their bodies in a way that has never been done before. However, as useful as talent is for your sporting career, it doesn't guarantee you success.

Einstein, one of the most gifted people to ever live, said, "Genius is 1% talent and 99% hard work" (Good Reads, 2019). What did he mean by this? First of all, Einstein wasn't saying that talent isn't an important factor to mastery, but instead, it wasn't the main driving force to success. As gifted as Einstein was, it was his sheer commitment to solving scientific problems facing the world that led to him making revolutionary discoveries. Moreover, it was Einstein's hard work that made it easier for him to develop his natural affinity for math and science. If he didn't put a lot of effort into developing his talent, he wouldn't have become a leader in his field.

Being a talented athlete doesn't hold much weight if your talent isn't nurtured with hard work. In other words, having the natural ability to play a sport doesn't mean that you don't have to put effort into developing your performance. To be the best in your team, you must couple your talent with an insane work ethic. While talent may give you a competitive edge against other players, it is only hard work that will guarantee how much progress you make in your career.

THREE TIPS ON HOW TO IMPROVE YOUR WORK ETHIC

The good news is that whether you are talented or not, you can achieve success in your career if you put in the work. Your aim should be to work harder than other players in your team and make the extra sacrifices that will put you in a league of your own! Here are three tips on how to improve your work ethic.

1. Get Out of Your Comfort Zone

The comfort zone is the familiar environment or lifestyle you have become accustomed to. You will know you are in your comfort zone when your daily tasks and routines stop being challenging. For instance, if you can go through a gym session without breaking a sweat, it means that your workout is no longer challenging. The danger of staying in your comfort zone is that it doesn't allow any growth. Everything feels safe and familiar, which eventually leads to low or barely any improvements in your performance. You can get out of your comfort zone by switching up your routines and exercises every once in a while and increasing the intensity of your training.

1. Become Passionate About What You Do

It is nearly impossible to put in extra work doing something you don't enjoy. You must develop a love for the sport you are playing so that the extra hours you spend developing your skills don't feel torturous. A great way to become passionate about what you do is to ask yourself why you do it in the first place. For instance, you can ask yourself:

- Why do I play this sport?
- What does it mean to me?
- What am I willing to do to succeed in this sport?

Admiring the sport you play and the journey toward becoming the best player in your league is what will help you persevere through grueling workouts and keep you focused on achieving the goals you set for yourself.

2. Set High Standards

One of Ronaldo's teammates from his old club Juventus, Blaise Matuidi, said that after the team won a match against Manchester United, the entire team decided to take a break and celebrate their win. Instead of resting, Ronaldo decided to train. Matuidi asked Ronaldo, "Aren't you tired? Don't you need to take some time to recover?" Ronaldo responded, "I was recovering the whole night and now I'm training. Being Cristiano Ronaldo I need to do this." Ronaldo had set high standards for himself and didn't compromise on them even when he had won a victory. He knows that being a high-performing athlete comes with the cost of working incredibly hard, despite how well you might think you are doing.

To increase your work ethic you must set high standards for yourself. This means deciding on the values, principles, and rules you are willing to live by, and ensuring that you stick to them. For example, if you have told yourself that you are going to eat healthy meals during the week, you cannot compromise your eating schedule when faced with temptation. Of course, at the beginning, maintaining your high standards won't be easy because it requires a lot of self-discipline. But each time you say, 'No' when met with temptation, you train your mind and body to honor your standards.

CHAPTER 2

BRING YOUR A-GAME

If mental health can bring somebody as big and as strong as me to my knees, then it can bring anybody to the knees.
— Tyson Fury

WHAT DO YOU BELIEVE?

The late Kobe Bryant who retired as a professional NBA basketball player came up with what he called the Mamba Mentality, which was a term to describe the kind of mindset athletes need to push past mental and physical barriers. In an interview, Kobe Bryant defined the Mamba Mentality as the ability to focus on the process of improving your skill while trusting in the fruits of your hard work.

To adopt Kobe's Mamba Mentality, you need to have a mindset shift.

Mindsets don't just come about out of nowhere. They are informed by our belief systems. A belief is something you regard as being true. This 'truth,' whether positive or negative, ends up shaping how you see yourself, the way you relate to others, and the kinds of habits and behaviors you adopt. Your beliefs are commonly formed through lived experiences, inferences, or the conclusions you draw about certain events. For example, your home environment growing up, what you were told by your parents, or the conclusions you have drawn about how others have treated you in the past, can be factors that inform your beliefs.

When you accept negative information about yourself or others as truth, it can lead to limiting beliefs that make you doubt your potential or make you feel intimidated by the journey of becoming successful at what you do. Limiting beliefs can also lead to self-sabotaging behaviors like procrastination, overthinking, or the inability to follow through with the tasks you set for yourself.

Even though you can't change your past experiences, you can update your belief system so that it aligns with the quality of life you desire. Updating your belief system will also make it possible to focus on the process of mastering your craft.

YOUR MENTAL HEALTH IS EVERYTHING

About 46.6 million Americans are living with a mental illness (Kuik, 2019). This means that one in five adults is suffering from conditions like anxiety, chronic stress, or depression. Just because athletes are competitive and work hard to achieve their goals, doesn't mean that they are immune to poor mental health. In fact, the pressure that comes with performing at a professional level can lead to many athletes experiencing mental illness.

Poor mental health is common among young athletes, particularly those in college or university. The pressure of having to attend class, pass grades, and also make time for training can be challenging for their mental health. According to Athletes for Hope, over 33% of college athletes experience symptoms of anxiety or depression, and among this group, only 30% end up seeking help (Kuik, 2019).

Athletes find it difficult to seek help due to the heroism that many people associate with being a successful sports player. Let's face it—when you see your favorite player shooting goals or displaying technique on the field, you can sometimes think they are invincible. They become somewhat of a role model that you look up to, even though they are human just like you. To maintain this heroic perception, athletes hide their battles with mental illness and try by all means to live up to the expectations of their coaches and fans. Fortunately, sportsmen like Tyson Fury have chosen to tell their stories about their mental health battles in hopes of ending the stigma about mental illness.

If you follow boxing, you will certainly know the name Tyson Fury. The British professional boxer is a two-time world heavyweight champion and has inspired many with his dedication to personal development and being outspoken about his battle with poor mental health. During the late months of 2015, Fury won his first world heavyweight title in a match against Wladimir Klitschko. Winning this fight was something he had always dreamed of, and finally, it was happening!

However, his victory also implied something else—now that he had achieved the pinnacle of success in his career, there was nothing left for him to work toward. Shortly after the fight, Fury fell into a deep depression. For the next 18 months he was suicidal and felt like there was no point in living. He had crossed off all of his goals and bought all of the cars and houses that money can buy. Despite having a family and amassing so much fortune, he didn't find anything to live for.

During his state of depression, Tyson Fury turned to harmful coping behaviors to avoid entertaining his negative thoughts. He began drinking alcohol excessively to the point of developing alcoholism. In an interview he did with Showtime Sports, Fury said "When I had a drink, it made the pain go away. Not pain as in physical pain but pain as in the longing and the repetitive thinking, day-in and day-out, that won't go away" (Turnbridge, 2020). His alcohol abuse quickly turned into drug abuse, which worsened his mental health and brought along severe consequences, such as having his boxing license revoked after failing a drug test.

The tipping point for Tyson Fury occurred in 2016 when he nearly crashed his car into a bridge while driving at 190 miles per hour. It was a planned attempt at ending his own life, but seconds before he could, he thought about his family and decided to pull over to the side of the road and reassess his life. Fury owes his recovery to his family, prayer, and love. Over the course of the next few years, he set new goals for himself— one of them being to reclaim his boxing license. He got back into the gym to shed over 100 pounds of weight he had gained during the darkest period in his life. Eventually, after paying millions of dollars in legal fees, he was able to reclaim his boxing license and get back into the ring.

Today, Tyson Fury is sober, strong, and has a clean bill of health. After 15 years of early retirement, Fury has made his boxing comeback at 54 years old. Nonetheless, his comeback hasn't taken away from his work as an advocate for mental health and sober living. He is perhaps one of the strongest men in the world, yet his life story teaches us that heroes are human too and that anyone can suffer from poor mental health.

HOW TO REPLACE NEGATIVE BELIEFS ABOUT YOURSELF

How many times a week do you remind yourself of your limitations? Are you guilty of having thoughts like these:

- I'll never reach that kind of level.
- I'm not strong enough to compete.
- There are so many athletes who are better than me.
- How could I make such a silly mistake?
- I'm lazy.
- I don't do enough to succeed.

These are just some of the common ways in which athletes talk down to themselves. It may seem like a form of encouragement to perform better, but it isn't. Encouragement is supposed to be uplifting, not discouraging. Speaking negatively about yourself can worsen your mental health. It can make you vulnerable to stress and anxiety or, in extreme cases, lead you down the path of depression. This is because what you believe about yourself has far greater implications on your self-worth than what other people may believe about you.

For instance, if you believe you are strong and capable, you are more likely to endure intense training or, at least, encourage yourself through it. But if you believe that you are weak or undisciplined, the chances of you surviving intense training are slim to none. Since your beliefs influence your thoughts, behaviors, and actions, thinking poorly of yourself can sabotage your efforts of becoming a successful athlete. Tyson Fury's battle with depression was triggered by what he believed about himself. After winning the most anticipated boxing match of his life, he believed there was nothing more to his boxing career. Was this true? Absolutely not, but despite it not being true, it was enough to lead him down the rabbit hole of depression and addiction.

While you can't control having negative beliefs, you can become more aware of them, allowing you to immediately replace them with empowering beliefs. There is a three-step process you can follow to replace your negative beliefs: Gain awareness, challenge validity, and shift your focus. Below is an explanation of each step.

1. Gain Awareness of Your Negative Beliefs

The first step to gaining more control of your negative beliefs is to notice whenever they come to mind. For instance, you may be at practice and feel inadequate compared to your teammates. At that moment, you should stop, take a moment to gather yourself, and determine what kind of negative belief might be informing your feeling of inadequacy. This is how you gradually gain awareness of your negative beliefs and the various contexts in which they arise.

Exercise: Close your eyes and think back to a time when you felt insecure about your performance. Try to remember the emotions you felt rushing through your body as these thoughts of inferiority plagued your mind. You may have felt worthless, jealous, or not good enough. Lastly, think about the kind of negative belief that may be hiding behind those feelings of inferiority. Can you think of something someone said or something you experienced that created this negative belief?

2. Challenge the Validity of Your Negative Beliefs

The second step is to confront your negative beliefs. What good is being aware that you have negative beliefs if you aren't going to confront them? Remember that your negative beliefs aren't based on facts. Rather, they are based on your perceptions about what is true in your life. This means that your negative beliefs can be false assumptions, bad judgments, or self-critical ideas you have about yourself and others. For example, thinking that you are the worst football player in the world is an exaggerated assumption that isn't based on facts. Challenging the validity of your negative beliefs requires you to seek factual evidence. When you can't find factual evidence, it means that your negative beliefs aren't worth holding onto.

Exercise: Recall a negative belief that you hold in your mind about your performance as an athlete. It could be a negative belief related to your physical or mental fitness, your level of skill, or your achievements thus far. Next, ask yourself this question: Are there any facts that prove this belief to be true? In general, you should be looking for at least three facts that support your belief in order for you to regard it as being true. If you can't find three facts, then it means your belief could be a false assumption, bad judgment, or self-critical idea.

3. Shift Your Focus

The final step is to shift your focus away from your negative belief. After you have proven that it is false, avoid ruminating on it and allowing it to fester in your mind. Of course, your negative belief won't immediately leave as soon as you realize it is false. It takes time for your mind to unlearn beliefs that it has harbored for many years. Nevertheless, your aim should be to find a positive belief or assumption to focus on instead of your negative belief. Make sure that what you choose to focus on has as much power to influence your mind as your negative belief. For example, if you previously believed "I am not fit enough to run a marathon," your new belief should be "I can do anything I put my mind to."

Exercise: On a piece of paper, write down your desired results related to your fitness, performance, and ability to succeed in your sport. Under each desired result, write down the positive belief that you can frequently remind yourself of whenever you feel discouraged in those various areas. In other words, these new positive beliefs will become the default beliefs you turn to when you want to shift your focus.

CHAPTER 3

MAKING SACRIFICES AND FINDING THE RIGHT BALANCE

How we function when no one is looking will shape who we are. The choices we make behind closed doors and the daily action we put towards our future shape our life, trust, and faith!
— Bethany Hamilton

DON'T LET ANYTHING GET IN YOUR WAY

In October 2003, surfer Bethany Hamilton headed to the beach to catch some waves—something she had always done when the weather conditions allowed. On this particular day, she was accompanied by a few close friends. The sun was out and the water was clear so the group did what they knew best, which was to ride the waves.

Meanwhile, heading toward them was a large tiger shark, the size of an average car. The group of friends noticed the shark when it was too late to make an escape, and unfortunately, Bethany Hamilton was attacked. The shark gripped onto her arm and pulled her body back and forth. The attack only lasted for several minutes, but when the chaos had subsided, Bethany's arm was missing.

Her friends made their way to her and hoisted her on a surfboard, calmly pulling her to the shore. When she arrived at the nearest hospital, Bethany had lost 60% of blood, so doctors rushed her into surgery to perform an emergency operation so they could save her life. For the next three weeks, Bethany recovered in the hospital but she desired to get back in the water.

After being attacked by a shark, most people would vow to never enter the ocean again, but this wasn't the case for Bethany. She was passionate about surfing and couldn't imagine her life away from the water. She reportedly said, "If I don't get back on my board, I'll be in a bad mood forever" (Surf Today, n.d.)

Twenty-six days after the shark attack, Bethany was back in the water learning how to surf with only one arm. A few months later, she was training for local competitions. Two years after the incident, Bethany won a national title, and since then, she has claimed several awards and is recognized as one of the leading female surfers globally.

FIVE THINGS YOU NEED TO SACRIFICE TO GO PRO

To succeed at something, you must be willing to make sacrifices. Speak to any professional athlete, and they will tell you how many other goals or experiences they have forfeited to reach the level of success they have. Bethany Hamilton, for example, is recognized as one of the best female surfers in the world. However, to reach her level of success, she has risked losing her life in the water.

The iceberg analogy clearly shows the nature of success. The achievements that are visible to the public make up 10% of the iceberg above water. This small portion is what people usually think success is made of. For example, when we think about a professional athlete's success, we remember the milestone victories, awards, and luxurious lifestyle. While these achievements are great symbols of success, they don't show the full picture.

Hidden under the water is the remaining 90% of the iceberg. This portion of the iceberg represents the part of success that most people don't see. In most cases, it is made up of the many sacrifices successful people need to make in order to achieve their goals. Sleepless nights, loneliness, financial troubles, injuries, and failures are the things that build success. Commenting about the hidden sacrifices people make to get to the top, podcaster David Perell said, "We see trophies, not sweat. We see diplomas, not homework. We see performances, not rehearsals" (Oppong, 2020). When we study the lives of great athletes, we are only looking at the 10% above the surface. What we don't see is the many years of commitment and hard work that have made their journeys look like overnight success.

Take a moment to reflect on your sporting career thus far. Think about the minor and major sacrifices you have made to get ahead. What opportunities have you had to turn down or tough decisions have you had to make to ensure nothing gets in the way of you and your dream? Here are examples of the sacrifices you will need to make to become a successful athlete:

1. Sleep

Professional athletes understand the importance of time and seek to maximize the 24 hours they have in a day. The more time an athlete spends on training, the better their performance will be on the field. It's common for athletes to wake up in the early hours of the morning, between 4 a.m. and 6 a.m., to start their first workout of the day. Waking up that early means getting to bed before 10 p.m. (earlier than most people) and waking up when everyone else is still sleeping.

2. Celebrations

When your goal is to become the best in the game, sports must be your number one priority, and everything else comes second. There will be times when you can't attend celebrations because they conflict with your training or match schedule. In a survey released by Oakley about the demands of being an athlete, half of the athletes who responded said they trained on their birthdays and 40% have played their sport on special holidays, like Christmas (Mens Health Staff, 2021).

3. Sex

On top of giving up your weekends and missing important celebrations, another sacrifice you will need to make is the amount of sex you have. Although having sex is healthy, it can affect an athlete's performance. Lower levels of testosterone during training or matches can lead to low energy and decreased strength. The no-sex rule is particularly important before competitions to enhance an athlete's levels of testosterone during the game.

4. Money

There is a myth that every athlete who makes it to the major leagues ends up becoming rich. Of course, there have been thousands of athletes who have made millions playing professionally, but not all athletes will become millionaires. The amount of money you make as an athlete is based on several factors, like your level of experience and the team you are playing for. Since it is so difficult for athletes to sustain their careers for over five years, playing sports may not always be lucrative.

5. Diet Choices

Do you have a sweet tooth? Well, you may need to cut back on how many chocolates you eat. Diet is a major factor determining an athlete's level of physical fitness. Along with training, athletes need to follow a strict diet plan to consume the correct amount of fats, proteins, and carbohydrates. Many of the foods you enjoy that aren't healthy will need to be cut back, including fried foods, baked goods, and soda. Your new diet plan will also dictate what times you eat and how large your food portions are, so prepare for an increased appetite!

FINDING BALANCE IN YOUR PERSONAL AND PROFESSIONAL LIFE

Succeeding as an athlete requires a lot of sacrifices, but that doesn't mean it should become your sole purpose in life. Remember that playing sports professionally is a career choice. Outside of your career, it is important to make time for rest, friends and family, and make time for other goals, like completing your college degree. It can be hard for young athletes to strike the perfect balance between their personal and professional lives. After all, to advance professionally, athletes are expected to dedicate a lot of time to their sport.

Since being an athlete is such a unique career choice, how you achieve balance in your life will look different from other people. Here are three things to consider when finding the ideal balance between your personal and professional life:

1. Accept Your Idea of Balance

Achieving balance looks different for each person. Some people require more time with family in order to feel balanced, while others don't need to spend as much quality time with family to achieve balance. If you want to determine what balance looks like for you, think about five of your core values and rank them from highest to lowest priority. Here is an example of a list of core values ranked from highest to lowest priority:

- Faith
- Work
- Training
- Friends
- Self-care

These core values will help you organize your time so that the things you value most are given the most priority in your life. This is how you end up achieving balance. Using the core values mentioned above, the top three values (faith, work, and training) would become daily rituals or routines. The remaining two values (friends and self-care) could feature once a week or twice a month. You may even have other desires or goals that you value that aren't part of your top five list. These desires or goals would need to be scheduled in advance so you can fit them into your calendar.

2. Realize That Balance Starts in the Mind

Creating balance in your personal and professional life doesn't stop at choosing what to invest your time in. Balance begins in how you feel about the way you spend your time, the tasks you are doing, and the perceived pay-off you are getting from your actions. An employee who works in a demanding job and doesn't find any pay-off in what they are doing may feel like the personal sacrifices they are making to keep their job aren't worth it. This would cause them to feel a work-life imbalance. However, if the same employee changes jobs and finds work that feels meaningful and brings a lot of pay-offs, they won't feel like their job is too demanding.

Bringing it back to sports, how you feel about your sporting career and the investment you are making to succeed has a lot to do with whether you will feel a good work-life balance. If you are dedicated to what you do and are willing to make the personal sacrifices to develop your skills and performance, your sporting career won't feel too demanding. In other words, you will be able to feel a healthy balance between your personal and professional life. Therefore, the balance you are looking for begins in your mind, in the significance you attach to your sports.

3. Be Honest About Your Limitations

No better person knows what you need than yourself. If you listen to your body, you will be able to identify and respond to your needs and acknowledge your limitations. Don't fall into the trap of thinking you are invincible. Even the greatest athletes of our time knew what their limits were. Achieving balance is about being honest about what you need in each moment or what you don't have the capacity to do in each moment. There will be mornings when you are supposed to be up at 4 a.m. for a morning jog but your body would rather spend a few more hours resting. Instead of forcing yourself to get up and go on the jog, the better option would be to give your body the rest it needs. Not only would this give your body the time to repair and recharge, but it would also boost your overall energy and performance on that day.

Ranked 13th in the world, the 24-year-old tennis champion Naomi Osaka has been known to value her downtime. When asked about how she maintains a work-life balance, she said, "Tennis is my job, similar to how a normal person has a 9-to-5 job. When I'm off the court, everything relaxes, and I don't really care that much about what I do or what I say" (Cohn, 2018). By treating tennis like a 9-to-5 job, she is able to spend time on other interests and endeavors off the tennis courts. A useful habit to learn as you progress in your career is to leave sports on the field, gym, or swimming pool and make a smooth transition to the roles you play in your personal life. Yes, training and eating healthily is important, but so is spending quality time with loved ones and having fun every once in a while!

THREE TECHNIQUES TO ORGANIZE YOUR BUSY LIFE

Time is your most prized possession. The more time you have on your hands, the easier it is to balance your personal and professional life. However, since you only have 24 hours in a day, maximizing your time requires you to implement certain time management techniques that will help you keep up with your daily tasks. Here are three techniques to help you get started:

1. Daily Planner

A daily planner is a calendar that helps you organize your daily tasks and commitments. This can be useful when you have to split your time between school, training, meetings, and special events to remember. You won't need to make a mental note of your schedule when you have it already written down. Your daily planner will tell you what you need to do and where you need to be at various times of the day. There are plenty of digital planner apps, like Todoist, Cozi, and Wunderlist that can help you manage your daily tasks. You can also opt to go the traditional route and purchase a daily planner at your nearest stationery store.

2. Time Blocking

Time blocking is a tool you can use on digital calendars like Google Calendar or iCal. You create "time blocks" for certain activities so you can get a visual idea of how your day is scheduled. In between activities you will have free blocks that you can use to rest or engage in side projects or interests. Time blocking trains you to put your time to good use. When you are scheduled to perform a certain task during a block, you give the task your undivided attention. You can also choose to organize tasks during times when you are most alert or energized. For example, you can block out your mornings for training and focusing on school work, and your evenings for resting and catching up on your favorite TV shows.

3. Pareto's Principle

Pareto's principle suggests that 20% of the tasks you do each day will result in 80% of the results. In other words, only two out of 10 tasks will offer you the highest rewards. Look at the activities you have scheduled for each day. Out of all those activities, which ones fall under the 20%? These activities should be prioritized above the other 80% of items on your schedule. Even if you only get three or four activities completed that day, if they fall under the 20% most valuable activities, you would have made 80% progress. Every once in a while, audit your schedule to see how many trivial tasks are filling up your time. Try to simplify your life as much as you can by removing tasks that don't add value.

CHAPTER 4

FAMILY CULTURE

You must learn how to hold a team together. You must lift some men up, calm others down, until finally they've got one heartbeat. Then you've got yourself a team.
— Paul "Bear" Bryant

WHAT IS A TEAM CULTURE?

In team sports, like basketball, football, or hockey, a sense of camaraderie amongst teammates is key to the success of the team as a whole. When players are at odds with each other, or spread negative beliefs amongst each other, it can dampen the team spirit and lead to low morale.

Have you ever played for a team where the players were divided? If so, how did you feel about attending training sessions or competing in matches? The lack of support from your teammates not only affected your mindset but may have also affected your performance during games.

The best approach when creating a sense of unity amongst teammates is to create a team culture. Team culture is built when players share the same values, beliefs, and interests about the team. Each player on the team commits to putting in their best effort at achieving the shared vision of the team. In other words, teammates adopt a 'We' mentality where individual progress is seen as contributing to the team's success.

Imagine you took a carpenter, politician, lawyer, and doctor and asked them to solve a building problem. How effective do you think they would be at working as a team? The only person who would have the experience, technical knowledge, and correct mindset would be the carpenter because they are used to solving building problems all of the time. The rest would add their input here and there, but wouldn't be as effective in finding the right solution.

Similarly, when players who have different attitudes, beliefs, and motivations join a team, there is a disconnect between them. Even though their goal is the same—to contribute to the success of the team—there aren't any shared expectations that unite them. Creating a team culture helps players find commonalities between each other and helps them focus on achieving mutual goals.

There are healthy and unhealthy team cultures. For instance, some teams have a highly stressful and demanding team culture where players are expected to risk their well-being to achieve team goals. There are also some teams where only a number of high-performing players are given attention, while the rest of the players are expected to assume a supporting role. These are both examples of harmful team cultures that can divide, distract, and in extreme cases, destroy a team.

The Janssen Sports Leadership Center provides eight examples of team cultures—six of them being unhealthy (Janssen, n.d.).

1. The Corrosive Culture

A toxic culture where teammates are constantly arguing with each other leads to division and tension on and off the field. Eventually, the trust and unity amongst players erode and individuals form smaller alliances within the team. It is usually these smaller alliances within a team that result in the breakdown of the team. Players can also become hostile to each other or the coach and resist following team rules.

2. The Country Club Culture

Think of the kinds of people who are members of a country club. They are successful, hard-working individuals whose sole purpose is to relax and have fun on the golf course. In a sports team, the country club culture is created when talented players feel entitled to special treatment because of their position or experience. Their motivation is to put in the least amount of effort while enjoying the perks of being part of an elite team. In these kinds of teams, there tends to be little accountability and barely any emphasis on performance and achieving results.

3. The Congenial Culture

A team with a congenial culture focuses more on players getting along with each other, rather than players achieving team goals. The coach or players work on creating a harmonious environment, to the extent that poor performance is often overlooked. The team becomes a source of encouragement but doesn't work as hard on winning and getting to the top. High-performing players on the team may feel unsupported in their desire to compete and become the best.

4. The Comfortable Culture

In a comfortable team culture, mediocrity is the order of the day. Players aren't pushed to their limits or expected to continuously make progress. In most cases, these teams end up staying in the same league, with the same ranking, for many years. When players feel challenged by new training regimens or different goals, the standards are dropped to ensure that no one feels uncomfortable. The coach or players make decisions that would be reasonable for everyone, rather than making decisions that would be best for the success of the team.

5. The Competitive Culture

Competitive teams are goal-driven, which is great! However, achieving results becomes the main priority of the team, at the expense of the well-being of players or cultivating relationships between players. Even though the competitive spirit is supposed to be directed toward opposing teams, it tends to spread within the team as well. Players can become distrustful of each other or see each other as rivals. They may compete for core positions on the team, playing time, or the coach's attention. Highly competitive teams aren't able to work together on common goals, since each player wants to be the "man of the match."

6. The Cut-Throat Culture

When a team prioritizes results over everything, it can create a cut-throat culture. The value of a player is seen in the kinds of results they can get. Players who don't produce results are often alienated, criticized, and threatened with a termination of their contract. Making mistakes in this kind of culture is seen as a sign of inadequacy or a topic of ridicule. The expectations for players are incredibly high and failing to meet these expectations isn't an option. Relationships between players aren't cultivated because they aren't as necessary for the team's success. Therefore, smaller alliances within these teams can form, which causes division amongst top-performing players and players who need more support.

7. The Constructive Culture

Teams that can balance achieving high-performance and cultivating relationships amongst players create a constructive culture. Even though the goal is to win, the team understands that winning requires unity and collaboration between players. Every member of the team is committed to working toward the team's success and will, therefore, work as hard as they can to contribute to this success. Collective effort is praised rather than individual effort. This reinforces the importance of players supporting one another.

8. The Championship Culture

Teams that make it to the highest leagues in their sport tend to have a championship culture. A strong mission and purpose are created by the coach and players, and this gives players something to work toward. Not only is each player clear on what they need to achieve, they understand the ways in which they need to improve their performance in order to achieve it. In other words, each player takes accountability for their role in helping the team succeed. Relationships between players are seen as crucial for the success of the team. Players are encouraged to build strong bonds, on and off the field, and offer each other the support they need.

Even though team culture looks different for each team, there are four basic components that summarize a strong team culture:

- The belief in the value of the work they are doing.
- The belief in the method for achieving common goals.
- A good balance between personal and professional life.
- Shared values amongst players, such as honesty, respect, and accountability.

Take a moment and think about how well your current team believes in the work they do, the method for achieving common goals, the balance of personal and professional life, and the importance of shared values. Your findings will indicate how much work you need to put in as a team to align your beliefs, passions, and goals. Ideally, you would want a team culture built on positive energy, where each player supports and holds each other accountable. You would want to feel a brotherhood or sisterhood amongst your teammates and look forward to working with them to achieve the desired outcomes.

Even if your team culture is already strong, there is no harm in deepening the bonds between you. If you would like to develop an even stronger team culture, ask each player on your team to answer the following questions on a piece of paper:

- What are the five values you would like to establish as the pillars of your team?
- What attitudes about your sport, team, and teammates do you need to have in order for your team to succeed?
- What goals would you like your team to work toward?
- What kind of atmosphere do you desire to experience during training sessions and competitions?

After everyone has completed their answers, go around the room asking each person to read what they have written. The coach or one of the players can be assigned the task of writing down everyone's answers, sorting them into four columns: values, attitudes, goals, and atmosphere. Finally, look for recurring ideas in each column and write them down on a separate list. These recurring ideas will help you identify shared values, attitudes, and goals the team has. These shared interests can be used to build or strengthen your team culture.

HOW TO BUILD A WINNING CULTURE

Having a team culture is only the starting point for succeeding as a team. Beyond coming together as players, each player must also adopt a winner's mindset. The winner's mindset is the kind of thinking that can help players overcome obstacles and achieve their goals. They shift their mindset so that winning becomes a possibility, not a mere fantasy. The winner's mindset takes players from fantasizing about winning to actually taking steps toward their goals.

Winning at sports or in life requires one fundamental factor—a positive attitude. A positive attitude is what keeps players in the game long enough to witness positive results. Any player can feel motivated at the beginning of their sporting career, but after two or three years into the journey, without seeing any tangible results, players can easily feel discouraged. A positive attitude nurtures personal development, so that even during challenging times, teams are able to have a positive outlook on their ability to succeed.

Think of any champion in the sporting world, and I guarantee you they have a winner's mindset. How do I know this? Because champions have a few things in common with each other: they persevere during tough times, relentlessly pursue their goals, and aren't afraid of stepping out of their comfort zone. These qualities aren't things that each champion is born with. Developing these qualities requires a conscious effort to change your mental attitude. American football coach, Dabo Swinney, said, "To be an overachiever you have to be an over-believer" (Liles, 2021). Adopting the winner's mindset is about increasing the faith you have in yourself and your team to push past challenges and reach your desired goals. Without this faith, you will struggle to endure the journey to the top.

New Zealand's national rugby team, the All Blacks, is one of the most successful sports teams in the world. Since its conception in the early 1900s, the All Blacks have won 78% of their test matches and three Rugby World Cups. Coaches, players, and even leaders from other industries have scratched their heads, wondering how this prolific team does it—how have they made winning a norm?

In his article titled, *15 Leadership Lessons from the All Blacks*, Todd Zipper identifies 15 principles the All Blacks use to win victories and perform at their peak level (Zipper, 2017). Below are five of the main principles mentioned in the article. As you read through each principle, consider how well your team exemplifies it.

1. Character

Character describes how a person thinks and behaves. Having the right character in team sports is about thinking and behaving in ways that would strengthen the team as a whole, rather than promoting individual interests. The All Blacks are a good example of players willing to make self-sacrifices for the advancement of the team. The players also place an emphasis on humility, asking questions like, "How can we improve on this?" They understand that small changes in character can lead to major shifts of attitude and mentality, which would benefit the team.

2. Adapt

You might be wondering how one team can win three World Cups. The secret to the All Blacks' worldwide success is their ability to adapt and evolve. After coming third place during the 2003 Rugby World Cup, the team went through a major restructuring. The coach at the time, John Mitchell, was replaced with Graham Henry, whose main task as new head coach was to improve the All Blacks' team culture. Henry's plan had four parts to it: improve team performance, create a vision for the future, eliminate players who will get in the way of achieving team goals, and ensure that each player has a self-adjusting plan on how they will contribute to the overall team vision. These changes brought about a considerable improvement to the team culture and led to one of the most successful periods in All Blacks history. Eight years after their 2003 loss, the All Blacks won the 2011 Rugby World Cup.

3. The Philosophy of Whanau

In Maori, Whanau means to be born, and it is often used in the context of relationships one cultivates with one's family or group of friends. The All Blacks strongly believe in being supportive of each other and enforcing peer-to-peer assessments so that they can help each other improve. They understand that poor-performing players end up sabotaging the success of the entire team; thus, it is in the best interest of each player to support other players' personal development.

4. Responsibility

Every rugby player who has ever played for the All Blacks has taken responsibility for their performance on the team. None of the players have left it up to the coach to push, motivate, or hold them accountable for their work ethic. Instead, the team's leadership provides a vision and a set of goals, and the players choose the best ways of achieving those goals. This means that each player enjoys a degree of autonomy or power to advance the objectives of the team, which causes them to display more commitment to the success of the team.

5. Rituals

Indigenous tribes across the world rely on rituals to keep the community united and to preserve common values, beliefs, and practices. Part of the reason behind the All Blacks' success is their use of rituals to create a strong team culture. If you have ever watched the beginning of an All Blacks game, you would have seen the team perform their famous ritual known as the Haka. The Haka is a ritual dance borrowed from the Maori tradition that is performed before each match begins. Not only is this dance meant to intimidate the opponents, but it is also a demonstration of the brotherhood among team players.

Looking at these five principles, it should come as no surprise that the All Blacks have remained successful for over a century.

Winning is more than a goal for these players—it is a standard they have set for themselves. As a result, the team is able to achieve extraordinary victories and maintain its position at the top of the rugby hierarchy.

THE NEED FOR A SOLID SUPPORT NETWORK

While athletes have the ability to do remarkable things with their bodies, they are still human like the rest of us. There are days when they don't feel like waking up early, eating healthy food, or playing a match. It can be a struggle for athletes to maintain high performance consistently, especially when they are feeling stressed or lacking support from peers, coaches, or family.

Becoming a professional athlete takes many years of training, and even after you have gone pro, there is still a lot of training you need to do to maintain your elite position. Let's face it—you won't always feel motivated to put in the work and time required for you to be the best. This is why you need something more sustainable than motivation to keep you going, such as a solid support network.

A solid support network is made up of individuals who you trust to help you achieve your personal and professional goals. With so many responsibilities on your shoulders, you need to have people in your corner who you can reach out to for psychological, financial, or spiritual support. These people could include family members, friends, mentors, or your local religious leader. Having this network of people by your side can make the grueling journey of becoming a successful athlete feel less stressful, lonely, and/or discouraging.

Take a few minutes to think about the kind of support you need in this phase of your sporting career. Do you need any of the following things:

- Encouragement
- Someone who can listen to you vent
- Unconditional love
- Someone to make you laugh
- Mentorship

Reflect on your needs and think about an individual in your life who has the capacity to fulfill that need. You may find that one person is able to fulfill more than one need for you. For example, you may have a parent who can offer you unconditional love and mentorship. If you can't find anyone within your network who can fulfill any of your needs, you can look outside your network for coaches, counselors, and leaders who can fill the gap. In this technological age, you don't necessarily need to know a coach personally to engage with them online, through videos, podcasts, or on their social media pages. Therefore, if you commit yourself to expanding your network, you will find the support you need.

It is important to learn how to ask for what you need. For instance, after identifying a parent, friend, or community member who can fulfill your need, you can approach them and ask if they would be able to offer you specific support that you need. Before approaching them, make a list of what exactly they can support you with so you can clearly express what you need. Don't be discouraged when someone isn't able to help you; see it as a redirection to someone who can!

You can also receive support when you make yourself available to support others. Your teammates, for example, can be a great source of support on your journey. Your willingness to support them on their journey will encourage them to support you on your journey too. Here are a few ways you can begin showing your teammates support:

- Reassure teammates that you are available if they need to talk.
- When a teammate is talking to you, focus on what they are saying and listen without interjecting.
- Acknowledge other teammates' experiences, even if you don't share the same point of view.
- Don't assume that your teammates are confident or feeling strong all of the time. Show compassion on and off the field—you never know which teammate is having a rough day.
- If you are unable to help a teammate with an issue, refer them to someone who can. As much as you would like to assist everyone, there are some matters that need a qualified coach or counselor.

CHAPTER 5
SETTING AND ACHIEVING GOALS

I am the greatest, I said that even before I knew I was.
— Muhammad Ali

GOAL-SETTING FOR ATHLETES

Any individual who is growth-oriented will have several goals that they are working toward at any particular time. Simply put, goals are the aspirations you are determined to achieve. Instead of leaving your dreams to chance, you consciously prepare for them to manifest in your life.

Goal-setting is, therefore, the deliberate process of planning out your goals. This process can help you define, create, and evaluate your goals so you have a better chance of achieving them. During the goal-setting process, you get to think deeply about what you want and what you are prepared to do to accomplish your desires. In other words, you will need to assess the mental, physical, and emotional investment you need to make to transform your life.

Like anyone who desires to achieve success, athletes spend a lot of time setting goals and working toward them. One of the key areas where athletes set goals is in their performance. For instance, an athlete may set a goal to improve their strength, endurance, or technical skill. Achieving their performance goal would give them access to greater opportunities, like playing for an experienced team. A performance goal is only one type of goal an athlete can set. Its job is to help the athlete increase their level of personal achievement, such as improving their physical strength. Since the focus is on the athlete's physical or mental needs, performance goals tend to be subjective in nature.

Another type of goal is an outcome goal. Here the focus isn't on the athlete, but on the benefit that personal success can have on others. For example, an athlete can set intentions to improve team culture and build better relationships with teammates. Although the athlete would be responsible for achieving this goal, the team would reap the most benefits from it. Other examples of outcome goals include winning a match, advancing to a higher league, or heading to the championships.

The third type of goal is a process goal. Similar to a performance goal, a process goal focuses on helping the athlete achieve personal success. However, instead of seeking to improve on performance, like being stronger and faster, the athlete focuses on the process of improving performance, like increasing the number of repetitions, carrying heavier weights, or practicing breathing techniques. In other words, the athlete works on increasing the quality of execution as a way of improving their overall performance.

Without goal-setting, an athlete has an idea of what they want to achieve, but doesn't have the necessary strategy to help them execute their goals. Goal-setting is what bridges the gap between mind and matter. For example, when you get inspired to do something, the inspiration comes in the form of a positive thought. Even though your thought gets you excited, it cannot bring about change in your life if it remains a thought. You need to find a way to move it from a thought level to a substance level. This can be achieved through goal-setting.

The difference between athletes who set goals and those who run on inspiration can be seen in the quality of their performance. Here are a few benefits that you will see when you start practicing goal-setting:

- **You will experience a boost in motivation.** Motivation is a fleeting emotion, meaning that it tends to come and go. However, when you set goals for yourself you create several milestones that help you sustain your passion and momentum for extended periods of time. Once you reach one milestone, you are motivated to work toward the next one, and then the next, until you achieve your desired goal.

- **Your level of self-confidence will sky-rocket.** The higher your goals, the more time, energy, and personal sacrifices you will need to make. However, pushing yourself to your limits has an incredible way of building your self-esteem. Your personal victories, regardless of how small or large they are, will improve the way you look at yourself. You will discover that there is truly nothing impossible for you to achieve!

- **You will enhance your performance.** An athlete's main goal is to improve their performance because that is what gives them a competitive edge. When you set goals for yourself, you can focus on specific areas of improvement so that your weaknesses become your strengths.

FIVE STRATEGIES FOR GOAL-SETTING

Believe it or not, there is a formula for effective goal-setting. And yes, it involves more than just setting "S.M.A.R.T" goals. Below are five strategies you can remember when practicing goal-setting:

1. Write Your Goal in Specific, Realistic, and Measurable Terms

The kind of language you use when setting goals is important because language clarifies exactly what you want to achieve and what you will need to do to achieve it. Specific goals are often easier to achieve than abstract goals. The difference between the two is the level of focus you are able to achieve. For example, writing down, "To be the best sports player in my college" is too broad and doesn't give you much to focus on. You can make this goal more effective by being specific: "To receive the award for Best Goalkeeper at the end of the year."

You can also test to see whether your goal is realistic. Realistic goals are goals you are capable of achieving with the resources you have available to you. For example, setting a goal to receive an award for Best Goalkeeper is only realistic if you already play for the position of goalkeeper. If you are a striker on your team, it wouldn't be realistic to aim for the best goalkeeper award.

Lastly, your goal must be measurable. This means that you need to include some sort of metric that will help you assess if you have achieved your goal. Examples of metrics could be achieving a certain body weight, being able to lift a certain number of weights in the gym, or running for a certain number of miles. You can assess your progress by looking at how close you are to reaching your chosen metric.

2. Set a Reasonable Time Frame

Setting a goal to run 10 miles doesn't mean much when a time frame isn't put in place. If you were to leave this goal open-ended, you could spend the next five years training to run 10 miles. Time frames give your goals structure. When you know that in a week, month, or year's time you will be expected to have accomplished a certain goal, you will know how to pace yourself and invest the necessary amount of time and energy. Nevertheless, your time frames must be reasonable. In other words, you need to assess how long it would take for you to develop a certain kind of skill. If you need indications of how long it will take to achieve certain goals, you can ask your coach, training instructor, or mentor.

3. Create Moderate Goals When You Start Out

Neither easy nor difficult goals will keep you motivated to succeed. However, this doesn't mean you need to stay in your comfort zone either. You need a certain degree of challenge to keep the fire within you burning, but not too much that you feel overly worked or ill-equipped. Moderate goals will push you out of your comfort zone and motivate you to improve on your performance. You will also feel confident in your ability to accomplish the goal, which will make it easier for you to stay committed in the long run.

4. Practice Writing Down Your Goals

Using a pen and paper to write down your goals may be the traditional method; however, it has been proven to be effective in setting and achieving your goal. When you write something down, your brain uses more energy to focus on whatever you are writing. This causes your brain to automatically assume that whatever you are writing down must be important to remember. Thus, goals that are written down tend to be more memorable than goals you think about. You can use a journal to write down your goals and keep track of the progress you make while working toward them. Ensure that your written goals are simple, moderate, time-based, and measurable.

5. Ensure Your Goals Match Your Desires

It is common for athletes to have different goals, even if they are playing for the same team. Goals are personal in nature; they respond to the individual's needs and wants. When setting goals, ensure that what you are striving for is what you deeply desire, not what your coach or family desires for you. Setting goals that match your desires will make the journey of attaining them feel less arduous and stressful, but more rewarding. You owe it to yourself to manifest your personal sporting dreams.

THE IMPORTANCE OF SELF-BELIEF

When you think of the phrase, "I am the greatest," which sporting legend comes to mind? Muhammad Ali, the legendary world heavyweight champion, repeatedly told himself, opponents, and reporters how brilliant he was. On the surface, this could have easily been seen as an ego trip, but his powerful words became a self-fulfilling prophecy.

Words have a powerful effect on the subconscious mind. Your words are rooted in the quality of your thoughts, which end up forming your belief system. For instance, if I were to spend a week with you and simply analyze how you speak about yourself and others, it would tell me everything that I need to know about your beliefs.

An athlete's belief system is one of the predictors of their success. Who they believe they are and what they believe they can achieve can set the tone for an athlete's career. Think of a belief system as being the foundation of a house. Even though you cannot see the foundation, the whole house is stabilized by it. If the foundation were to be removed, the house would collapse. In the same way, a belief system is what keeps you grounded in your goals and helps you find balance between who you are and what you do. Your beliefs can set the tone for your work ethic, relationships with your coaches and teammates, the quality of your diet, and achieving balance in your life.

Self-belief is an asset for an athlete. We can define self-belief as the individual's belief in their ability to complete a task or achieve a goal. Muhammad Ali is a good example of an athlete who believed in their ability to succeed and become the world's greatest boxer—and so he did! Since he believed that he was the greatest sports player to ever live, his thoughts and actions changed to correspond with his belief. In other words, his talent and skill as a boxer improved the more he affirmed his own greatness. Subconsciously, Muhammad Ali was manifesting his dream of becoming a world champion when he repeatedly affirmed the positive beliefs he had about himself. Speaking highly of himself also made fans respect him and opponents fear him.

Take a moment and think about your belief system. What kinds of beliefs do you have about yourself or your ability to achieve your goals? If you were to repeat these beliefs consistently, would you feel encouraged or discouraged? If you have beliefs that encourage you to become a better person, they are worth strengthening through positive "I am" affirmations, like Ali's "I am the greatest." However, if some of your beliefs cause you to have doubts about your ability to succeed, take time to challenge those beliefs by determining whether they are based on facts or assumptions. If they are based on assumptions, you can easily replace the negative assumption with a positive one. For example, if you assume you will never be a great basketball player because you aren't tall enough, draw up a list of all the average height basketball champions in the world and study their rise to the top.

Lastly, you can practice affirming the positive qualities, talents, and skills you have. Hearing yourself speak about your strengths will give you a boost of confidence and make you eager to set more challenging goals. It will also give you the competitive spirit that every successful athlete needs to succeed.

Muhammad Ali's words shaped his sporting career and activated the Law of Attraction. Have you heard about the Law of Attraction? It is a universal law that suggests that you attract what you think. If your thoughts are mostly negative, you may start behaving or negatively reacting to life, thus reinforcing your negative thoughts. The same applies to positive thinking. Your positive thoughts cause you to look at life from an optimistic perspective, and you may start behaving or positively reacting to life.

What does the Law of Attraction have to do with goal-setting? The kinds of thoughts you have about your ability to succeed can influence your outcomes. If you think that you are going to get an injury, you send out a negative message into the universe that causes you to attract a negative result. The result may not be a physical injury, but it can be another negative equivalent, like being benched for a few matches in a row or being replaced by another player.

Therefore, when setting goals, ensure that you improve your thought life to match the quality of the goals you desire. If you desire to improve your running speed, for instance, avoid entertaining doubts about your physical fitness. Match your goal with positive thoughts about your ability to succeed, and affirm the positive qualities that can help you achieve your goal. For example, when your goal is to improve your running speed, envision yourself running a mile in the shortest amount of time. In your mind, repeat the phrase, "I have the power to achieve my goals." Enhance the positive vision with an affirmation, such as "I am victorious in everything I do," or "I am getting faster each day."

CHAPTER 6

FOCUS ON WHAT YOU CAN CONTROL

You really can't worry about stuff you can't control... You need to focus on getting where you need to be and not worry about what could have been and what should have been.
— Robbie Lawler

DON'T WORRY ABOUT YOUR GAME

In the world of mixed martial arts (MMA), Robbie Lawler, often nicknamed "Ruthless" Robbie, is a force not to be reckoned with. The former UFC welterweight champion has had a successful career winning bloody fights, one opponent at a time. However, what makes him a remarkable fighter isn't his ruthless alter ego inside the cage, but his calm and nonchalant demeanor outside of the cage.

Throughout his 20 year career as a professional athlete, Lawler has remained level-headed about his victories and humble about his reputation as a fighter. In an interview with Bleacher Report, he told a journalist, "I just do what I do. If the fans enjoy it, they enjoy it. If not? Oh well. It's just how I fight and who I am, but it's cool to be recognized as a good fighter and a guy who puts on a show" (Taylor, 2020).

When asked about his violent strategies inside the cage, Lawler simply adds, "That's just the sport I play." Interestingly, his motivation to become a legendary MMA fighter isn't about winning championships, but the process of becoming a mentally and physically stronger athlete. He explains, "I enjoy working on aspects of myself, fine-tuning stuff, and just tweaking skills and techniques. Just trying to constantly evolve" (Taylor, 2020).

Robbie Lawler's outlook on his sporting career helps him differentiate between his persona in the ring and his attitude outside of the ring. When competing, his focus is on playing the best he can, not worrying about what spectators may think about him. Moreover, his goals are performance and process-related, meaning they center around improving his talent and abilities as a player, rather than maintaining his reputation as a champion.

WHAT IS WITHIN YOUR CONTROL?

It's very rare for an athlete to sustain a 20-year career, like Robbie Lawler, but after reading about the MMA fighter's outlook on his career, it is clear why he has been able to remain in the game for so long. Lawler's secret is simple: Focus on what is within your control, and forget about the rest.

The more successful an athlete becomes, the easier it is for them to become distracted by things that don't really matter, such as building a strong fan base or getting recognition from other experienced athletes. In many cases, these distractions are things the athlete has no power over, meaning they cannot change or manipulate external outcomes. For example, an athlete isn't responsible for choosing their fans; instead, it is the fans who are responsible for choosing an athlete. Therefore, when an athlete is preoccupied with the number of fans they have, they are focusing on something they have no influence over.

Imagine your brain had a limit to the number of thoughts it could hold in a day. Let's say that within a space of 24 hours, your brain had the capacity to entertain 1,000 thoughts. Now that is extremely little considering that the average human being has 6,000 thoughts a day. Nonetheless, with your limited number of thoughts, you would be forced to think about ideas that add value to your life, your to-do list, positive beliefs about yourself, and any other thought that can make you feel good about your day. It wouldn't be wise for you to dwell on negative thoughts that bring you down or situations in your life that aren't turning out as you had hoped.

Unfortunately, this thought limit doesn't exist and you are free to entertain both positive and negative thoughts. However, it doesn't hurt to be conscious about the quality of your thoughts. Your attitude and emotions are determined by what you spend most of your time thinking about. Do you desire to be more productive? Then you need to think a certain way. For instance, spending your morning setting positive intentions and looking at your to-do list will help you become productive during the day, but complaining about the inconveniences in your environment or thinking about the tasks blocking you from being productive won't bring about a productive attitude.

The same goes for when you desire to win in your competition. Think about the kinds of thoughts you would need to have to develop a winner's mindset. Perhaps you would need to have confidence in your strengths and believe in your team's ability to win. These thoughts would trigger positive emotions that can be your source of fuel during the competition. Worrying about your opponents' tactics would have adverse effects and cause you to become timid during the game.

Focusing on what is within your control is about reclaiming your power and reinvesting it in the things that you can change. One of the most powerful things within your control is your thoughts. Believe it or not, you can control whether you think positively or negatively about yourself, your sporting career, your teammates, and others. You have the power to turn what worries you into something that brings you hope. You can also redirect your attention from a troubling situation that isn't working out as planned to a positive situation that brings you a sense of peace.

Take a moment to think about some of the thoughts you have allowed free entrance into your mind. While a few were positive, I am certain others undermined your self-worth, made you feel like a victim of life, or reminded you of your weaknesses. As overpowering as these thoughts may seem, they are still under your control, meaning you don't have to put up with them if you don't want to. You can confront your negative thoughts and replace them with empowering ones that can help you achieve your dreams.

REGULATING YOUR MENTAL STATE

Maintaining a positive outlook on life isn't as simple as thinking positively. There are so many distractions that come into your life to steal your time, attention, and lower your mood. Being aware of these distractions can help you regulate your mental state despite the circumstances you may face.

What are some of the distractions that negatively affect your mental state? Below are three to consider:

1. Information That Wastes Your Energy

You have a limited amount of energy to use in a day. As an athlete, most of your energy is spent on training or preparing for competitions, but there is also mental energy that you spend browsing social media, reading tabloids and blogs, or listening to people. Energy is wasted when it is spent unproductively. For instance, when you read negative reviews about yourself or you surround yourself with pessimistic people, you waste valuable energy and put your mental state in jeopardy. The better approach would be to spend time reading inspirational content, listening to people who have value to add to your life, or better yet—shutting down social media and enjoying a few hours of silence.

2. Information That Makes You Paranoid

Paranoia is a mental condition that causes a person to entertain delusions of being targeted by someone, being the subject of unwanted jealousy, and thinking more highly of themselves than is healthy. Paranoia can only be diagnosed by a mental health practitioner, like a psychologist; however, some of the common symptoms of paranoia include:

- The inability to trust others
- Being easily offended
- Making negative assumptions about other people's feedback
- Reacting instead of responding to another person's remarks

The information you expose yourself to can cause paranoia. For instance, when you spend too much time in your own mental world and dissociate from reality, you can find it difficult to accept how things actually are. You may give more importance to how you think and feel, rather than accept that not everyone around you, or on the internet, thinks and feels in the same way as you do. In other words, your perceptions of reality are valid, but they aren't necessarily the truth. How you see the world is subjective and isn't the only way to experience life. To achieve a healthy mental state, practice acknowledging other viewpoints, even if they are negative or go against what you believe. Remind yourself that other people are allowed to disagree with you or see things differently than you, and this doesn't mean they are against you.

3. Information That Doesn't Carry Potential Opportunities

Finally, your mental state can be compromised when you preoccupy yourself with information that doesn't improve your quality of life. Here's a simple rule to remember in life: If it doesn't make you happier, healthier, or richer, it's not worth thinking about! For example, does worrying about the economy add more dollars into your pocket? No, it doesn't. Neither does worrying about catching a disease, incurring an injury, or not being chosen to play in your dream team. Any kind of thought that doesn't bring potential opportunities is a wasteful thought, which eventually affects your state of mind.

The best way to regulate your mental state is to focus on the things within your control, as well as the things that add value to your life. For example, envisioning a positive future is not necessarily within your control, but it does add value to your current life. When regulating your mental state, it is also important to be intentional about each thought, asking yourself questions like, "Is this thought worth entertaining?"

Now that you know that your thoughts can compromise your mental state, it is worth considering the kind of things worth thinking about.

Let's begin with social media. Are comments left by fans worth thinking about? The answer is yes and no. Not everything you see on social media is worth your time or energy because social media is built on the opinions of others. Since you have no power over the opinions of others, social media content is not worth thinking about. However, getting a positive message from a fan can add value to your life by giving you a boost of confidence, so be selective about the content you choose to engage with.

Next, let's consider your sporting career. Is it worthwhile to think about your hopes of being chosen to play for a specific team or getting a certain position on a team? Once again, the answer is yes and no. Remember that you can't control how a coach perceives you or the position you are assigned on a team. Your role on a team is decided by the team's leadership and their vision for the team. In other words, don't take it personally when you are not selected to be a part of a team or play in a certain position—it isn't a 'you' thing, but a 'them' thing. Nonetheless, even though you don't have control over being selected by a team, you can aspire to play for a specific team and use that goal to motivate you to work harder.

As you have found in these two examples mentioned above, deciding on what to focus your attention on usually has a positive and negative effect. When assessing the value of a thought, weigh the pros and cons of it and allow that to help you make your decision. In general, you want to focus your attention on the things you have control over that also bring net positive effects. In other words, you want to entertain thoughts that you have the power to positively influence and that bring mental, physical, or emotional health benefits in your life.

With that being said, here are three things that are within your control and are worth thinking about:

1. Breathing

Breathing only requires you to inhale or exhale, but the pace of your breathing is worth thinking about. The rhythm of your breathing regulates your heart rate and stress response. When your breathing is calm, your mind and body are often relaxed too. However, when your breathing is irregular, it can accelerate your heart rate, bring tension to your body, and make you feel anxious.

The next time you find yourself in a stressful situation, instead of seeking to change the situation (which is probably out of your control anyway), focus on slowing down your breathing, taking deeper and longer inhale-and-exhale breaths, and returning to a calm and consistent rhythm. Not only will doing this deactivate the stress response, but it will also help you shift your mental focus from anxious thoughts to calming thoughts.

2. Self-Talk

The perception you have about yourself is more influential on your personal development than the perception others have of you. Throughout the day, your inner voice makes commentary of how you are performing certain tasks or whether you are making good decisions or not. The commentary made by your inner voice is called self-talk. When your self-talk is encouraging, you will have the courage to take action on your goals. You will feel as though you have an inner cheerleader supporting you in every choice you make. However, when your self-talk is discouraging, you can end up sabotaging your own efforts, procrastinating, or giving up on yourself. The same inner voice becomes a tyrant, making you feel inferior, ashamed, fearful, and not deserving of opportunities.

Start noticing how many times you speak poorly about yourself. Make a tally of each time you have a negative thought about yourself, and at the end of each day, count how many negative thoughts you had. Do this for at least a week, each day tallying how many times you have negative self-talk. The more conscious you are of your self-talk, the easier it will be to anticipate or catch negative thoughts before or as they happen, and replace them with positive ones.

3. Gratitude

Gratitude is recognizing the good in everything around you. As an athlete, you will face many highs and lows, but you don't need to define yourself by your highs or your lows. Instead, you can find the good in every experience you have, whether it is positive or negative. Remember that you can't control what happens to you but you can control how you perceive each situation. Gratitude will help you see things from a positive perspective and focus more on the lessons learned, rather than the failure incurred.

Practicing gratitude can be as simple as saying thank you when you receive help or guidance from a person. However, it can also become a daily practice, like writing down five things you are grateful for each day. You can show gratitude for small and large blessings in your life, like being greeted by a stranger with a warm smile or signing a major contract with a sports team. No one has a perfect life, but those who are thankful for their lives wouldn't trade it for anything!

YOU CAN'T CONTROL YOUR REPUTATION

One of the pressures young athletes face is the pressure to be accepted by others and the need to build a good reputation. Of course, we all know the power of a good reputation. Being well-known and liked by others can open many career opportunities and get you ahead in life. However, as valuable as a good reputation is, it isn't something you have control over.

A reputation is the summary of what other people think about you. The feelings and attitudes they have about you are based on their preconceived ideas and beliefs. In other words, people's perceptions of you are based on their unique worldview, belief systems, and experiences in life, not anything you have done or failed to do.

Since your reputation is built and torn down by others, it isn't something you can control. You can't control how proud your community is of your accomplishments, how impressed your coach is with your hard work, or whether people actually value the amount of dedication you have to your sport. Knowing that you have no control over your reputation should be liberating because it means that you cannot be lifted up or brought down by what others think of you. In essence, you reclaim full ownership of your narrative and how you think of yourself, and other people's opinions come secondary to that.

If you have followed tabloid news over the years, you may have seen many professional athletes whose reputations were destroyed after cheating allegations, drug scandals, and other reputation-killing stories released in the media. In just a matter of hours, they went from being praised by fans and sports companies to being ridiculed and stripped of their endorsement deals. Those athletes who had defined who they are based on their reputation suffered severe mental health issues as a result of being shredded into pieces by others. However, those who were able to separate themselves from their reputation were able to make a comeback.

Receiving praise from others can make you feel good about yourself, but you should never internalize praise to the extent that it shapes who you are. The same people who you accept praise from can be the very people who criticize you and make you question how you see yourself. It is recommended to practice seeing yourself from your own eyes, through the narrative you have created for yourself. Other people can call you great but it matters most what you believe about yourself.

Think for a minute about the stories you hold about yourself. What kinds of stories do you tell yourself about your physical fitness? The relationships with your teammates? Or your sporting career? Your stories have the power to shape your goals, standards, and experiences. For instance, if you believe that you have an incredible work ethic, you are more likely to work hard without needing support or motivation. Your story is what causes you to wake up early in the morning and go for a jog, followed by an intense workout in the gym. Your story is also what determines how much you push yourself, regardless of your coach's requirements.

The stories you have about yourself should be determined by you, not external forces. When they are controlled by external forces, like the opinions of other people, your goals, standards, and experiences can change based on the changes in your environment. For instance, when you receive validation from your coach, you might be motivated to work harder, but as soon as your coach stops offering validation, your performance drops. When your stories are dependent on external forces, they can also make you value your fame or reputation more than you value yourself. This means you allow external factors to determine your worth as an athlete, rather than determining your own sense of self-worth.

Therefore, whenever you sense that your narrative has been hijacked by external forces, you should check in with yourself and rewrite each story to align with your values, principles, goals, and beliefs. For example, it's not enough to tell yourself that you trust yourself. You need to reflect on the times when you allowed the opinions of others to drown your thoughts and feelings, and make an effort to stand up for yourself in public and private spaces. This is how you rewrite a story and reclaim power over how you see yourself.

CHAPTER 7

REWIRE HOW YOU THINK

Progress is impossible without change, and those who cannot change their minds cannot change anything.
— George Bernard Shaw

THE MENTAL SHIFT TO WEIGHT LOSS

Physical fitness is essential for a successful sporting career. When an athlete is out of shape, they cannot perform to the best of their ability. However, it can be difficult for athletes to maintain a consistent weight or consistent muscle mass throughout a season. Bad habits like overeating can lead to excessive weight gain, compromising an athlete's level of fitness.

In the late months of 2015, NFL player Eddie Lacy was publicly called out by his coach, Mike McCarthy, for piling on too much weight. The Packers coach said that Lacy's performance during the season had been negatively impacted by his steady weight gain. He also gave Lacy an ultimatum: lose the extra weight during off-season or face being fired from the team.

The announcement made by coach McCarthy caused Lacy a lot of public shaming on social media, with many people ridiculing his weight gain. However, Lacy didn't allow the negativity on social media to deter him from his goal of losing the extra weight and getting down to 240 pounds. During off-season practice, Lacy picked up several sports like boxing and basketball as a healthy form of exercise. He also committed to eating healthy foods, like lean chicken breast and salad, while his teammates feasted on pizzas, fried chicken, and spaghetti. He also tried P90X workouts, which are grueling 7 day home workouts that last between 1–1.5 hours per session.

After four months of working out and eating healthily, Lacy had allegedly lost 18 pounds, which got him down to 234 pounds, about 6 pounds under his target weight. Commenting on his experience losing weight and making healthy lifestyle changes, Lacy said, "It was different. Some things were harder than others. But at the end of the day, it's all about the result. Whether it's fun or not, you've just got to get it done" (Polacek, 2016).

REWIRING YOUR BRAIN THROUGH NEUROPLASTICITY

It is a myth that athletes don't develop bad habits. In fact, any human being with the capacity to make a choice can develop bad habits. Some habits can be broken without having to undergo a major intervention, while others can only be broken by rewiring the brain.

Much of what informs how you think, feel, or behave is stored in your subconscious mind. Your subconscious mind makes up 90% of your total brain function, meaning that what you have stored deep in your subconscious mind is more influential to how you see and experience the world around you than your conscious actions, like short-term decision-making or planning.

There are many reasons why you would need to rewire your brain, but the main reason is the desire to change your behaviors. Your subconscious mind is where your habits, belief system, long-term memory, and phobias are stored. When you notice yourself displaying destructive habits or self-limiting beliefs, it is an indication of what you have stored in your subconscious mind. Thus, rewiring your brain allows you to adjust your habits, behaviors, and beliefs on a subconscious level and adopt healthier habits, behaviors, and beliefs that can assist you in achieving your goals and living a healthier lifestyle.

Before going into the process of rewiring the brain, it's important to explain the adaptable nature of the brain. The kind of data you choose to feed your brain programs it to think a certain way. You may not be in control of the stimuli in your environment, but you have full control over how you interpret and make meaning of these stimuli. For example, your brain doesn't know the difference between good and bad habits. It processes the information you have given it and waits for you to instruct on whether a habit is pleasurable or harmful. You could be addicted to smoking cigarettes but your brain would only remember the calmness you derived from the first cigarette you ever smoked. This pleasurable feeling is what your brain recalls whenever you crave or smoke a cigarette.

The brain's adaptable nature also implies that it can replace negative behaviors with positive ones. This is good news because it means that you don't have to be stuck to your destructive habits and beliefs forever. You can give your brain a new instruction that allows it to accept new information and derive a different sense of meaning from it. Your brain's ability to change over time is known as neuroplasticity. Neuroplasticity describes the process your brain goes through when it is repeatedly exposed to behavior or experiences that become ingrained in how you think and see the world.

The thoughts, feelings, and behaviors you frequently engage with become stored as part of your long-term memory and are automatically encouraged by your brain. In other words, after taking 10–20 lessons with a driving instructor, your brain memorizes the process of driving a car so that it can automatically remind itself of the procedure whenever you get into the driver's seat. Therefore, repetition is the key to neuroplasticity, and what allows you to rewire your brain. The more you rehearse a thought in your mind, the stronger and more influential it becomes in what you do. The same applies when certain behaviors, like binging on food, are reinforced.

As easy as it is for your brain to absorb new information, unlearning information takes time. To enjoy the full effects of neuroplasticity, you need to engage in various mind strengthening exercises that can help you reinforce positive ideas, thoughts, and actions. Here are a few mind strengthening exercises that you can practice to progressively change how you think:

1. Brain-Boosting Activities

To facilitate the process of neuroplasticity, engage in activities that force you to think. There are many brain-boosting activities to choose from, like playing chess, doing a crossword puzzle, or solving riddles. Dedicate 15–30 minutes a day to an activity that will make you think and stretch your mind.

2. Find Ways to Be Creative

Creativity is good for brain health and learning new behaviors. It can trigger the release of feel-good hormones that decrease stress, enhance your mood, and even improve the function of your immune system. Creative energy can inspire you to look at your problems differently and come up with new solutions to address the challenges you are faced with. There are many different ways to be creative, like switching up your routine, engaging in arts and craft activities, daydreaming, or reading.

3. Visualize Your Long-Term Goals

In the story, *Alice in Wonderland*, by Lewis Carroll, the Cheshire Cat says, "If you don't know where you are going, any road will take you there" (Paton, 2016). This means that unless you have a clear understanding of the kind of lifestyle you desire, life can present you with many different options—most of them being options you wouldn't pick for yourself. It is, therefore, important for you to practice visualizing the future you desire so you don't leave it up to chance. Dedicate 15–30 minutes a day thinking about your long-term goals, in both your personal and professional life. As you reflect on your goals, ask yourself the following questions:

- What career milestones do I want to reach in the next five years?
- How can I improve my physical fitness in the long term?
- Which relationships do I need to nurture right now to build a strong support system in the future?
- What lifestyle habits do I need to adopt to achieve my long-term goals?
- What lifestyle habits do I need to eliminate to achieve my long-term goals?

Spending time visualizing your long-term goals will create a purpose within you that gives your life meaning and will motivate you to positively improve your mindset.

HOW TO BUILD HEALTHY HABITS AND BREAK UN-HEALTHY ONES

Have you ever struggled to break an unhealthy habit that was getting in the way of your performance? If so, then you have personally seen the effects of neuroplasticity! Like ordinary people, athletes struggle with bad behaviors too. However, athletes' bad behaviors can have serious consequences for their sporting careers. Take NFL player Eddie Lacy, for example, whose career was nearly cut short due to poor eating habits. The average person wouldn't lose their corporate job for putting on a few pounds, but an athlete's career is based on healthy eating habits and optimal physical fitness.

Therefore, as a young athlete, you will need to sit down with yourself from time to time and do a recall of your behaviors. Reflect on your lifestyle choices and the common behaviors you exhibit. Determine how your behaviors either hurt or help your sporting career. Next, think about the long-term effects of your behaviors on your mental, emotional, and physical well-being. Ask yourself: *If I continue on like this, how will my life turn out in five years?* For example, choosing to skip weekend practices may not seem to carry major consequences now; however, when your work ethic begins to drop after a few months, you can face much greater consequences, like not being selected to play for competitions.

Habits are as much about achieving external outcomes as they are about reinforcing the confidence and respect you have for yourself. In other words, your outward behaviors communicate how you inwardly feel about yourself. When you engage in harmful habits, it can be a sign of self-sabotage or having low self-esteem. Both of these signs may indicate underlying psychological issues that you need to speak to a counselor about, such as feeling anxious or insecure about your performance as a player. When you find yourself engaging in harmful behavior, you can ask yourself this simple question: *Am I honoring myself with this kind of behavior?* If the behavior doesn't honor who you are or who you aspire to become, then it is worth breaking that behavior.

So, how do you break harmful habits? In his book, *Atomic Habits*, author James Clear speaks about the five areas to focus on when you are seeking to break bad habits and adopt healthier habits (Clear, 2018):

1. Incremental Improvement

When most people think about breaking habits, they assume you need to go cold turkey, meaning completely eliminating the habit from your life. Going cold turkey isn't the most effective strategy because it can shock your body and cause uncomfortable withdrawal symptoms. The better approach is to wean yourself off the behavior by making small improvements on a consistent basis. While taking "baby steps" doesn't seem transformative, in the long run, those baby steps will compound and lead to changed behavior. Plus, your body won't go into shock or withdrawals during the process because you are changing your behavior at a comfortable pace.

2. Improve Your Systems

A system is a set of processes working together to produce a specific result. Your personal systems are formed by your beliefs and principles that help you structure your life and get things done. When you have weak personal systems, you may struggle to create structure in your life or hold yourself accountable for certain actions. When breaking unhealthy habits, your aim should be to review your systems and ensure they support the kind of lifestyle you desire. Go through your beliefs, principles, and standards you have set for yourself, one by one, and think of ways to hold yourself accountable to them. For example, if you believe that hard work is the key to success as an athlete, think of at least three different ways you can start holding yourself accountable to working hard. Do this for all of your beliefs, principles, and standards. In the end, you should have a list of small tasks you can do on a daily, weekly, or monthly basis to reinforce a healthy lifestyle.

3. Envision the Person You Desire to Become

Once again, the technique of visualization is mentioned. How can visualization help you break unhealthy habits? When you have a mental picture of who you desire to become, you feel an intrinsic motivation to make positive behavioral changes. Instead of breaking your habit to make your family, coach, or teammates happy, you are driven to break your habit so that you can become a better version of yourself. Visualize yourself living a healthier lifestyle, free from your harmful habits. See yourself reaching the next level of physical fitness and feeling confident in yourself. You can also envision how positive improvements in your sporting life will affect your personal life.

4. Shift Your Perspective

Take a minute and think about what attracted you to your unhealthy habit in the first place. For instance, if you have a habit of binge eating, think about what may have made the behavior appealing. Was it the pleasure you derived from eating your favorite snacks? The emotional comfort that food gives you? Or how binging allowed you to focus on something else, other than your current life circumstances? Figuring out what attracted you to your unhealthy habit can help you shift your perspective about the habit and make it unattractive.

For example, if you became dependent on playing video games because it was convenient and attractive, you can break your habit by finding ways to make it inconvenient and unattractive. To make it inconvenient, you can store your video console on the highest shelf inside your garage so that it is harder to reach. You can also make it unattractive by selling your video games so that you aren't enticed to play. The harder and less pleasurable you make a habit, the less rewarding it is for your brain. Over time, you will feel less inclined to perform the habit and, instead, adopt a healthier habit that brings more satisfaction.

5. Update Your Environment

The last area you will need to focus on when breaking unhealthy habits is your environment. For permanent change to take place, your environment should support your lifestyle changes. Think about it this way: How successful will you be at eating healthy food when your refrigerator and pantry are stocked with all sorts of candies, pastries, and desserts? If you truly wanted to change your eating habits, you would need to replace the unhealthy food options with healthier alternatives, and ensure you don't have access to junk food. The same applies when seeking change in your work (during training or at the gym), home, social, and digital environments. You need to remove any distractions, temptations, or barriers that can make it difficult for you to break free from your unhealthy habits.

CHAPTER 8

BUILD CONFIDENCE IN YOUR SKILLS

Being a superstar means you've reached your potential, and I don't think I've reached my potential as a basketball player and as a leader yet.
— Steph Curry

PUSH PAST THE CRITICISM

Steph Curry is a talented basketball player who plays for the NBA. He has achieved a countless number of awards and continues to shock fans with his impressive career statistics. But in high school, Curry was the basketball underdog that many scouts undervalued. He was mainly criticized for his athleticism, leadership, and ball handling on the court. In 2009, a scout reportedly said that Curry's athleticism was below standard and that he needed to do considerable work improving his ball-handling skills (Astramskas, 2015).

Instead of allowing the criticism to dampen his spirit, Curry focused on improving his skill and getting better with each match he played. As a freshman at Davidson College, he scored an average of 22 points in every game, which qualified his team to play in the Elite 8. And during the 2009 NBA Draft, Curry was picked by the Golden State Warriors to play as one of their guards—a decision the team never regretted, as Steph Curry later became their MVP (most valued player).

When asked about the naysayers who criticized his performance earlier in his basketball career, Steph Curry said, "No matter what people said, I always blocked them out and kept training. That dedication and commitment to the game I love, the long hours spent honing my skills one-on-one with my coaches, is what ultimately drove my success" (Astramskas, 2015).

WHY CONFIDENCE MATTERS IN COMPETITIVE SPORTS

To an athlete, confidence is the make-or-break factor. It separates the high performers from those who prefer to stay in their comfort zones. We can define confidence as having faith in something or someone. For example, an athlete can have confidence in their potential or in their ability to overcome obstacles. Having confidence allows the athlete to push themselves beyond their limits and achieve their goals.

Take a moment to think about where an athlete's confidence comes from. In other words, ask yourself what factors in an athlete's life can lead to self-confidence?

While many factors can contribute to an athlete's self-confidence, resilience, motivation, and laser-sharp focus are three crucial multipliers of confidence. As mentioned before, resilience is the ability to recover and pick yourself up from unexpected setbacks. Resilient athletes tend to have a positive attitude toward themselves and their lives. Instead of perceiving failure as a weakness, they take away the valuable lessons and work on developing themselves. Resilience builds confidence because it causes athletes to feel secure in who they are and who they are becoming.

Motivation is the second factor that leads to confidence. Here, we can split motivation into two different categories: intrinsic and extrinsic motivation. Intrinsic motivation refers to the personal satisfaction you receive from accomplishing a goal, whereas extrinsic motivation refers to the external rewards you receive from accomplishing a goal. When playing a certain sport is something an athlete is passionate about, they are more likely to endure through the highs and the lows of their journey to becoming a professional sports player. As tough as it may be to receive criticism or make sacrifices, the intrinsically motivated athlete still believes the journey is worth it!

On the other hand, when an athlete is motivated by the respect they will earn by playing for a specific team or making it to the highest league, they can also find a way to endure through challenging times. They may not be motivated by an inner desire or purpose, but that doesn't make the incentive any less meaningful. Both intrinsic and extrinsic motivation can build confidence in an athlete because they create an aspiration or dream the athlete can work toward fulfilling.

Lastly, having a laser-sharp focus can also build confidence. How? Focusing on a specific goal, like improving physical fitness, can limit the number of distractions around you. All of your physical, mental, and emotional energy is invested in one area of your life, rather than being split into multiple areas of your life. Concentrating your efforts in one area allows you to see noticeable improvements as time goes on. Over time, you gain confidence in that area as your level of skill and mastery increase too. It can be tempting for athletes to work on several goals simultaneously; however, juggling goals in this fashion can overwhelm the athlete and bring down their confidence. It is better to focus on a single task or goal and make incremental improvements until the task or goal has been achieved.

The two major killers of confidence are doubt and fear. Let's face it—the sporting world is extremely competitive. To become a professional athlete, you need to play better than some of the highest performing athletes in the industry. In other words, you don't compete with average folk, you compete with incredibly talented people who are gunning for the same position as you!

Having this pressure playing at the back of your mind can make you feel threatened by other great athletes or doubt your potential. Even though you are an amazing player, you might compare yourself to your teammates and believe that you are not as good as them. You may also experience anxiety each time you play because you don't want to make a mistake and have your coach or teammates question your talent as a player. Doubt and fear are real and when they aren't properly dealt with, can chip away at your confidence as an athlete. In many cases, the solution to eliminating doubt and fear is to strengthen your resilience, motivation, and level of focus.

At some point in your sporting career, you will experience a decrease in confidence. When this happens, realize that it is normal and common amongst athletes. Since you are playing a competitive sport, you are bound to feel insecure about your abilities or performance once in a while. Nevertheless, you never have to suffer from low self-confidence for an extended period of time. Here are five useful tips to raise your confidence:

1. Remember That You Are Your Own Worst Critic

How you speak about yourself can sound more harsh and judgmental than how others speak about you. Be aware of your self-talk and the tone or language you use when speaking to yourself. When you are tempted to criticize your own efforts, pause and consider whether you would speak like that to a friend or family member. Adjust your approach and style of communicating with yourself, and show yourself compassion because you deserve it!

2. Be Intentional About Thinking Positively

If your brain is accustomed to making negative assumptions or jumping to the worst-case scenarios when faced with challenges, you will need to consciously remind yourself to assume the best and think positively with each thought that crosses your mind. At the beginning, this may seem like an arduous process, but after a while, you will naturally develop faith in yourself and your ability to succeed in life, despite the challenges that come your way.

3. Give Yourself Permission to Dream

Having big dreams for yourself is not childish. Your dreams are what shape the outlook you have on your future and give you a sense of purpose. It is healthy to fantasize about your extraordinary long-term goals, even if they seem far-fetched to you right now. Dreaming will increase your level of motivation and make you focus on achieving your goals. Each morning before you get out of bed, or in the evenings before you go to sleep, lie down on your bed and close your eyes. Visualize a dream that you hope to fulfill in the next 10 years. Immerse yourself in the dream and experience it as though you were living in it.

4. Remember Your "Why"

Another useful tip that can raise your confidence is reminding yourself why you started playing sports in the first place. Behind every successful person is a strong 'why,' the purpose that drives their attitude, behaviors, and decision-making. During tough times, having a purpose can ground you and increase your resilience. Take a piece of paper and a pen and write down the answers to the following questions:

- Why did I choose to become an athlete?
- Why did I choose to play this sport?
- Why am I on this team?
- Why do I train as hard as I do?
- Why are the sacrifices I have made worth it?

Place your piece of paper in a safe place. Whenever you are feeling discouraged, pull out your piece of paper and remind yourself of the purpose behind your career choice and lifestyle.

5. Honor Your Word

If you desire to increase confidence in yourself, you must learn to keep your word. In other words, when you tell yourself that you will do something, ensure that you follow through and do it. It might seem trivial to delay or reschedule tasks, but subconsciously when you do this, you are creating a habit of not being accountable to yourself. It is better to set realistic expectations of what you can and cannot do, rather than setting high expectations and failing to accomplish your goals. When creating your daily task lists, for example, give yourself three tasks to accomplish. If you end up accomplishing more, great! However, if you only end up accomplishing three tasks, you will feel confident nonetheless.

OVERCOMING THE FEELING OF REJECTION

You can't escape rejection in life, and you certainly can't escape it in sports either. There will always be someone doing less than you and always someone who is doing better than you. I'm sure you can think of some athletes that you perform better than and other athletes who perform better than you.

When you are not chosen, praised, or acknowledged for your talent, you will feel a sense of rejection. Depending on how personal you take the rejection, it can feel as though the person rejecting you is turning their back against you. The feeling is worsened when the person rejecting you is a close friend, coach, or relative you desired acceptance from. For example, if you are looking for support from your parents and you don't receive it, you can feel deeply hurt. When it isn't addressed properly, the pain of rejection can follow you for the rest of your life and affect your self-confidence.

As part of the preparation to become a professional athlete, young athletes need to get comfortable with the idea of being rejected. If the world's best sportsmen and women were rejected hundreds of times before they made it to the top, you are likely to encounter the same kind of rejection on your journey to the top too. The rejection you face will come from people you know, as well as people you don't know—even the uninformed spectator who watches you compete can walk away feeling unimpressed with your performance.

Fred Bastie, the founder of a college athlete recruiting company, identifies three types of rejection high school athletes, in particular, encounter (Bastie, 2017):

1. Immediate Rejection

Immediate rejection occurs when a college coach or scout attends a high school game to scout for talent and approaches several athletes, except for you. That can be a clear indication that the coach or scout isn't interested in watching you develop your skill, at least not in the immediate future. Though disheartening, immediate rejection can help you manage your expectations and cross off colleges that aren't showing interest in you as a player.

2. Indirect Rejection

Indirect rejection is perhaps the most difficult to experience because you receive some attention from a college coach or scout, but not enough for them to take you seriously, offer you an opportunity, and engage in meaningful conversations. For example, you may have spoken to a scout after a game and they gave you their contact details, but after several attempts at emailing them, they never respond to you. Or maybe you get invited to a training camp that seems like the first step into getting accepted into a school, but after the camp, no further progress is made. Since this type of direction isn't blatantly obvious, it can make you feel confused and doubt yourself as a player. Once again, you need to manage your expectations when approaching coaches or scouts. If you don't hear a clear and affirmative, 'Yes,' then assume the answer is, "Not right now."

3. Direct Rejection

Direct rejection occurs when a college coach or scout acknowledges your talent or skill as a player, but after watching a few of your games changes their mind about you. The more invested you were in their approval, the more this type of rejection can hurt. For example, if you had already told yourself that you have found your new team, being rejected by the coach can feel like a personal attack. However, you should remind yourself that until you have signed a contract and formally entered a team, you are technically still auditioning for a spot. Furthermore, it is rare for a coach or scout to directly reject you based on your talent or skill. After all, it was your talent or skill that caught their attention. Their rejection is mostly due to the vision they have for their team, which your playing style or personality may not be a good fit for.

At the end of the day, rejection is rejection—it hurts regardless of how you look at it. However, instead of allowing the rejection you face to define you, you can learn from each experience and find ways to become an even stronger and faster athlete. Here are some of the tips you can remember when overcoming rejection:

- **Accept that even successful athletes get rejected.** There isn't an athlete in the world who is immune to rejection. All athletes, at some point along their careers, will face rejection. Getting rejected doesn't mean you aren't a good athlete, it simply means you are not a good fit for a particular team.

- **Ask for feedback from the rejector.** When a coach or scout rejects you, ask them to give you feedback on their decision. It can be uncomfortable hearing someone speak about what they see as your weakness, but this information can give you clues about the areas of your fitness or performance you need to work on.

- **Be honest about the amount of work you need to do.** True confidence comes from having a healthy self-perception. It lies in understanding both your strengths and weaknesses and being aware of how others perceive you. Learn to assess your progress and performance as an athlete in an honest way, being truthful with yourself about the areas you excel at and the areas you need to improve.

CHAPTER 9

HOW TO APPROACH A TRAINING SESSION AND COMPETITION

Luck has nothing to do with it, because I have spent many, many hours, countless hours, on the court working for one moment in time, not knowing when it would come.

— Serena Williams

HOW WINNERS TRAIN

When you think of American professional tennis players, whose name comes to mind?

Did you think of Olympic gold medalist and champion Serena Williams? The 23 Grand Slam singles title holder is by far one of the greatest tennis players in history. Part of her success is due to her discipline and work ethic during training.

What gives Serena Williams her X-Factor is her fierce serving style that allows her to swing powerful balls with a great amount of accuracy. Both Serena and her sister, Venus, were taught how to serve balls by their father. The trio would spend many hours in the court, practicing how to fire shots from all areas on the court. Instead of seeking to master every component of the game, Serena focused on improving her unique strength, which continues to give her a competitive advantage in how she plays. In her own words, "The older I get, the better I serve" (Tony Robbins, 2015).

Another admirable quality about Serena Williams that has made her successful over the years is the way she bounces back after failure. Back in 2007, the tennis champion suffered multiple injuries that caused her to lose her position as the number one player in the world and drop to the 172nd position by 2011. During her time in recovery, Serena struggled with bouts of depression, although after rehabilitation, she was able to regain her physical strength and get back on her winning streak, as though no time was lost!

In an interview with The National in 2012, Serena spoke about her attitude toward winning: "I really think a champion is defined not by their wins but by how they can recover when they fall. I have fallen several times. Each time I just get up and dust myself off and I pray, and I'm able to do better or I'm able to get back to the level that I want to be on" (Rizvi, 2012).

So whether it is mastering her unique strength to give her physical edge or adjusting her mindset so she can have a psychological edge, Serena Williams exemplifies an athlete who consistently works at getting physically and mentally tougher to achieve her goals.

TRAIN LIKE A WORLD-CLASS ATHLETE

There are a few qualities that world-class athletes have in common: skill, strength, and discipline. However, when it comes to physical build, no athlete is the same. Each sport requires a different physical build to succeed. For example, a wrestler will need to work on strength training to gain muscle while a track athlete will spend a lot of their time working on cardio to become lean and strong.

For you to succeed in your sport, you need to figure out what kind of physical build will enhance your strength, speed, or endurance. Some sports require more strength than speed, or more speed than endurance (think short distance running). Finding out what it takes for you to succeed in your sport will give you targeted goals to work on.

Now that you know what exactly you need to work on, you can prepare for your training. If you're wondering how many hours world-class athletes train per week, you are looking at between 15–20 hours. In total, that would be nearly a full day's worth of training! You are not expected to invest that much time on training as yet, although in the future that may very well become your routine too. Since you are still starting out, you can work toward training 3–5 times per week, for 20–60 minutes a session.

Here are a few more tips that will prepare you to train like a world-class athlete:

1. **Set goals for your training plan.** Before you start a training plan, you need to decide what areas of your physical fitness you are going to work on. This will ensure you have a structured approach to training and that each session is a step toward your overarching goal. If you are not sure what fitness goal to set for yourself, ask your coach, trainer, or teammates for feedback.

2. **Stick to a regular routine.** Setting and sticking to a routine will help you keep track of your progress and ensure that you are repeating certain workouts on a regular basis. Some sports require athletes to gain muscle memory in order to become stronger and build muscles faster. Repeating a specific routine, for a specific period of time, can make it easier to grow and maintain muscles.

3. **Remember to eat well.** What you eat during training is just as important as the workouts you do. Nutritious food supplies your body with the energy, nutrients, and minerals needed to achieve the physical build required for your sport. Each sport will have its own recommended diet plan, including instructions of what to eat or not to eat and the number of meals to consume per day.

4. **Listen to your body.** When starting out your training plan, it can be tempting to push your body to its limits. This is never a good idea because it can do more harm than good. When your body is tired, you need to give it sufficient rest so it can detox, repair, and replenish energy. When you get an injury, stop your workout immediately, and consult a medical practitioner.

5. **Don't skip recovery days.** Another common habit amongst athletes is to skip their recovery day, or rest day. You might feel up for another training session that day, but it's important not to overwork your body. Take the day off and spend it sitting in an ice bath, getting a back massage, spending 20 minutes in a steam room, or reconnecting with friends and family.

You can decide to follow a training plan you found online from a coach, athlete, or fitness guru, or better yet—create your own! The advantage of creating your own training plan is that you get to decide on the types of workouts you are going to do each week, how long each session will last, and how much you can push your body. However, more importantly, when you create your own training plan, you get to factor in your personal life and plan your workout routine around your personal commitments, like school, hobbies, and social events.

There isn't a one-size-fits-all approach when creating training plans; even athletes who play for the same team may have slightly different plans. Nevertheless, there are six components that are common amongst training plans, which can serve as your blueprint when you create your own plan. Here are the five components:

1. Endurance

Endurance training helps athletes build power and speed over a specific period of time. The most common exercises used to develop endurance are aerobic exercises, such as cycling, swimming, or running. Getting your weekly dose of endurance training can train your body how to conserve energy through rigorous activity for longer periods of time.

2. Movement

Regardless of the sport you play, you will need to strengthen your movement. Movement exercises improve how you handle and move your body so you can act with more precision and strength. Some of the fitness equipment that can help you work on your movement include treadmills, bike rollers, or stationary bicycles with controllable pedals. Another great way to improve your movement is to analyze video footage of some of your past games and observe strengths and weaknesses in your movement. Note down some of the footwork, handwork, or body movements you need to work on in your next training session.

3. Strength

The amount of strength training you do will vary depending on your sport. Some sports, like contact sports, require a great deal of strength training. But there are other sports where a lot of muscle mass is not needed. In general, the older you get, the more muscle mass you will start losing, so strength training becomes a greater priority for older athletes. When planning workouts for strength training, you can include movement exercises, core-strengthening exercises, and weight training.

4. Speed

While endurance is about staying active for a longer time, speed focuses on moving faster in each second. In sports like running where speed is necessary for winning, speed training will be incredibly useful. Fortunately, your main goal will be to increase the pace at which you complete certain workouts. For example, it might take you 15 minutes to run a mile, but your goal is to complete a mile within 10 minutes. Your training sessions would focus on increasing your running speed gradually, until you can comfortably run a mile in 10 minutes. Once you have achieved your desired speed, you will need to regularly maintain it by doing short speed drills once a week or a few times a month.

5. Recovery

The final component of every training plan is recovery. Recovery must be included in your training plan because it can help you improve your physical fitness. During your recovery days, your body repairs muscles and tissue, refuels energy, and relieves tension. It isn't necessary to have a structured plan on how you will spend your recovery days; however, you should never use them as "cheat days" where you binge on unhealthy foods. Recovery days should be used for relaxing the mind and body, lowering blood pressure, staying hydrated, and catching up on sleep.

These five components are simply indicators that you can build on when creating your training plan. Feel free to invest more time in certain components than others, as well as give yourself as many recovery days as you need per week.

HOW TO PREPARE YOURSELF FOR COMPETITION DAYS

Having a well-planned competition day routine is just as important as having a structured training routine. What you do leading up to the game, during the game, and immediately after the game will affect your overall performance. The most successful athletes in the world stick to structured routines on competition days. We can call their structured routines rituals because they are performed habitually, in the same process. The best competition day rituals focus on small tasks that can improve the athletes' preparedness for their game. Below is an example of what a typical competition day ritual would look like, from the morning, to after the competition:

1. Morning of the Competition
- Wake up
- Recite positive affirmations
- Full body stretches
- Drink a glass of water
- Shower
- Eat a healthy, full breakfast

2. Before the Competition Begins
- Arrive at the locker rooms and get dressed
- Do a warm-up with the rest of the players
- Eat a healthy snack
- Visualize positive outcomes for the competition
- Wait for the competition to begin

3. During the Competition
- Play the best that you can!

4. After the Competition
- Do a self-assessment of your performance during the game
- Get inside a hot/cold bath, drink plenty of water, and get some rest
- Eat a nutritious meal

- Spend quality time with your family
- Listen to a motivational video
- Get a good night's rest

Another often overlooked aspect of competition day is nutrition. While you should be eating healthily during the days leading up to your competition, what you eat on the day of your competition can affect your performance during the game. What you eat pre-competition, during the competition, and post-competition can help you in different ways. For example, before the competition, you want to eat foods that provide you with a good amount of energy, but don't leave you feeling full or tired. During the game, your priority will be to stay hydrated and keep your energy high. After the competition, you want to eat foods that can assist your body in the recovery process. So, let's take a look at what an athlete's typical competition day diet plan would look like:

1. **Morning of the Competition/Pre-Competition**
   - Lean protein (chicken, turkey, or duck breast)
   - Healthy carbohydrates (Green salad, various fruits, whole-grain rice, sweet potato)
   - Healthy fats (assortment of nuts, avocados, extra-virgin olive oil)
   - A few glasses of water

2. **During the Competition**
   - Drink plenty of water or sports drinks (beverages infused with electrolytes)
   - Snack on any fruit or seeds
   - Protein bar

3. **After the Competition**
   - Lean protein, healthy carbohydrates, and healthy fats
   - Recovery protein shake or healthy smoothie

CHAPTER 10

DEALING WITH SUCCESS AND FAILURE

I've missed more than 9,000 shots in my career. I've lost almost 300 games. 26 times, I've been trusted to take the game winning shot and missed. I've failed over and over and over again in my life. And that is why I succeed.
— Michael Jordan

RISING EACH TIME YOU FALL

Michael Jordan is not only a household name; it is also a brand. Behind this brand is a six-foot, six inches man, who has been listed in the Naismith Memorial Basketball Hall of Fame. There is no doubt that Jordan's professional basketball career was full of many victories; however, along the way, he has encountered failure.

In high school, Jordan was not picked to play for the varsity team because the coach believed he was too short (back then, Jordan was only five foot, ten inches in height). Instead, his coach placed Jordan in the junior varsity team so he could at least get more game time. At the time, Michael Jordan, who was only 15, was devastated at what felt like rejection. In an interview, Jordan recalls how he went home and cried for what seemed like an eternity, and he was ready to give up his dream of being a professional basketball player.

His mother encouraged him to get back on the court and improve on his performance. Jordan became the most hard-working player on his basketball team. In moments where he felt tired or restless, he would visualize not seeing his name on the list pinned in the locker room and that would give him enough motivation to continue working hard. Jordan kept his momentum going, and his impressive talent landed him a spot at the University of North Carolina, and eventually, becoming a player in the NBA.

Nowadays, when you think of the name, "Michael Jordan," you don't think of failure, do you? That is because Jordan used his setbacks as stepping stones toward his success. Not at any point did he allow himself to be defined by his momentary mistakes. He learned from them so that through failing, he could become a better person!

FAILURE CAN BE JUST WHAT YOU NEED

Life is unpredictable, which means that you are likely to experience both highs and lows in your sports career. The highs and lows are not what define you as an athlete; how you handle these highs and lows does. Your character is seen in how you pick yourself up from tough times, dust yourself off, and get back on the field or court. In five years' time, people won't remember the specific details of your mistakes, but they will remember how you handled them and came to a resolution.

Failure can, therefore, be a good teacher. It can reveal your blindspots, help you refine your goals, and learn from your mistakes. However socially, failure has become synonymous with weakness. This makes it hard for athletes to admit and accept failure. Since the sporting world is such a competitive environment, athletes want to show themselves as strong and invincible. However, by looking at failure as a teacher, rather than a weakness, it can be a lot less overwhelming for athletes to experience and overcome their failures.

How you respond to failure will prove how open you are to learning from your mistakes and becoming a better person. Each time you fail, you will be presented with two choices: you can either seek to understand what might have caused you to fail and work toward correcting your mistake, or you can take it as a personal attack on who you are and react defensively.

The healthy approach would be to see failure as an opportunity to grow and do things differently. Instead of defining yourself by your failures, you can take away the valuable life lessons you learned from not having your plans work accordingly. Ideally, failure should be something you welcome into your life, because unless you make mistakes every once in a while, you will never get the chance to develop your character, shift your mindset, and build resilience.

Below are some of the tips you can follow when you are processing disappointment:

1. Write Down How You Feel

What makes failure feel like your whole world is crumbling down are the strong emotions that are often experienced when you fail. You might feel angry, betrayed, worthless, or humiliated. Feeling these emotions is an uncomfortable experience, and most times it seems better to just suppress them. However, suppressing your strong emotions will only create a build-up of negative energy inside of you.

Therefore, after experiencing disappointment, take some time to write down how you feel. You can use keywords or write full sentences or paragraphs. Allow yourself to vent your frustration until you feel a heavy load lifted from your shoulders. Remember that sometimes, the situation may feel worse than it actually is. In other words, your strong feelings may not be an accurate representation of how severe the failure was.

2. Look for the Lessons

In every 'bad' situation, there is also an aspect of 'good' hidden in it. Changing your perspective on your failure can help you see it from another viewpoint. To challenge how you perceive your failure, complete this sentence:

If it wasn't for my failure, I wouldn't [add positive benefit].

When one door shuts, another door opens. This is the nature of life. When you shift your perspective on your situation, you might discover an opportunity in what looked like a hopeless situation.

3. Avoid Harboring on Negativity

Okay, so you have made a mistake—that makes you human! No one expects you to be perfect, so it is an unreasonable expectation to expect that from yourself. You won't always make good choices or have a positive mindset, that's normal. The only way to bounce back from setbacks is to forgive yourself for the poor choices you made and focus on moving forward with a positive attitude. Don't remind yourself of your character flaws or physical weaknesses. Look at your life as one big adventure of learning how to become a better version of yourself. Check your self-talk and make sure you entertain positive thoughts and beliefs about yourself and others.

YOUR BEST IS GOOD ENOUGH

Athletes are often told to be the best. However, being the best doesn't mean chasing after perfection. Perfectionism is a character trait that causes an individual to set high standards of excellence in various areas of their lives. Perfectionism can manifest in three different ways. You can set high expectations for yourself, expect excellence from others, or believe that those around you expect excellence from you.

Being a perfectionist can be both a blessing and a curse for athletes. On the one hand, it can help you push past your comfort zone and work diligently toward your goals. Although, on the other hand, being a perfectionist can cause you to sabotage your own performance by pushing yourself too hard and experiencing burnout.

Here are a few questions you can ask yourself to see whether you would be considered a perfectionist:

- Do you perform better during your training sessions than you do during competitions?
- Do you set high expectations for your performance during competitions?
- Do you feel like your teammates expect you to excel in each competition?
- Do you tend to worry about how your coach, trainers, or teammates think about you?
- Are you critical of your mistakes and indifferent about your victories?

- Do you have a hard time relaxing when you are not training?

If you have answered yes to most of these questions, you may be showing signs of perfectionism. Fortunately, there are ways to shift your mindset and become less strict or obsessive about your performance:

1. Learn to Trust Yourself During Training and in Competitions.

You can't control what happens around you, but you can regulate what happens inside of you. Learning to trust yourself can lower your anxiety on and off the field. It can help you do your best while also being aware of your physical limitations. Practice performing in a way that feels natural to you, without overthinking your techniques or giving yourself pressure to perform. Get to learn the difference between working hard and pushing your body too far.

2. Trust That You Will Survive Challenges

Another way you can use trust is by allowing yourself to fail, knowing that you have the strength and wisdom to learn from your failures. Accept that your journey to becoming a professional athlete won't always be smooth-sailing. You will encounter challenges from your personal and professional life, which will test your character and problem-solving abilities. Embrace the challenges and see them as necessary learning opportunities.

3. Work on Efficiency Rather Than Perfection

Your objective as an athlete should be to progressively improve your performance. The progress occurs over time, through the many training sessions and skills development you undertake. Seek to improve your performance with each competition and build up your skill, strength, and discipline gradually. Instead of attempting to have a perfect training session or game, focus on improving your execution.

MANAGING SUCCESS ONCE YOU ACHIEVE YOUR GOALS

There will come a time when you live the kind of lifestyle you have always dreamed of! You will wake up in the house of your dreams, playing for the best team in the highest league, and be in optimal physical shape. When you reach this level of success, your life will feel absolutely magical. However, in all this magic, you may lose sight of your purpose as an athlete and get lost in the lifestyle. Below are five things to remember when you finally achieve your career goals and live the life of your dreams:

1. Practice Self-Awareness

It is important to remember who you are in the midst of your success and growing popularity. Reminding yourself of who you are will protect you from being influenced by other people. Stay true to your values and principles, even when you find yourself in a room with people who think and believe different things than you. Developing self-awareness is the key to staying connected to who you are during life transitions.

2. Celebrate Your Wins

When you have accomplished a milestone, remember to celebrate the occasion! You deserve recognition for the incredible work that you do for your team and community. Rewarding yourself for hard work is a good incentive to help your brain reinforce good habits. After celebrating a win, you will be reminded of the reason you are on this journey in the first place, and why you ought to keep moving forward!

3. Maintain Professionalism at Work

While toasting to your victories is encouraged, getting caught up in your celebrations will eventually affect your performance. Do you remember the winner's mindset? It is focused, resilient, and goal-oriented. This is the kind of mindset you should have most of the time. During training and competition days, take a moment to get yourself in the zone. Remind yourself of your commitment to the sport and your team, and work as efficiently as you can. At all times, treat your coaches, teammates, and fans with respect and consideration.

4. Find Someone to Mentor

One of the best ways to express your gratitude is to find a way to transfer your skills and knowledge to someone climbing up the ranks underneath you. There might be a lot of people who look up to you and desire to reach the level of success you have been able to obtain. You can find a way to mentor these aspiring athletes and transfer the many lessons you have learned throughout your career. In doing so, you can leave a lasting legacy so future athletes can walk in your footsteps.

5. Maintain Balance Between Your Personal and Professional Life

The more successful you become, the harder it will be to balance your personal and professional life. Once fans, coaches, and teams start learning about you, they will expect to see and hear more of you. Nonetheless, being an athlete is only your career, not the center of your life. Be deliberate in making time for the people, hobbies, and side projects you love most. Learn to say no to job offers or any other kind of opportunity that might steal away time for rest, recharging, or being with loved ones.

CONCLUSION

You are your best asset. Do you know what that means? It means that you are the most valuable commodity in your life. When you are healthy and happy, everything else around you flourishes. If being an athlete is what makes you feel healthy and happy, then it is important to follow that desire and become the best athlete you can be! You owe it to yourself to spend the rest of your life striving toward this single, most important goal.

Throughout this book, you have read the stories of professional athletes who have faced different kinds of experiences on their way to the top. They have been through rejection, failure, mental health problems, and self-doubt—just to name a few. Nevertheless, their commitment to being a world-class athlete superseded their fears, and eventually, they were able to realize their dreams.

Perhaps what has become strikingly clear to you as you have read through the book is the importance of mental toughness. Without mental toughness, having talent or being a hard worker won't amount to much. This is because there are certain challenges where your talent or hard work won't be able to help you through. Only sheer faith in who you are and confidence in your purpose will ensure that you come out on top all of the time.

Since mental toughness is not something that you are born with, it is your job to find ways to develop your character and shift your mindset so that you can look at situations from an empowered point of view. Yes, this takes a lot of practice and willingness to break harmful habits and adopt positive ones that can improve your quality of life. However, if you are open to the experience, you will find the journey of developing mental toughness extremely rewarding.

Your sporting career is just beginning and you have so many productive years in front of you. Strengthen your talents, boost your work ethic, and assess your performance over time. If you ever feel fearful, rejected, or discouraged, remind yourself that your sports heroes went through the same trials and tribulations too. Your lows are just as valuable as your highs, and in hindsight, you will realize why everything had to happen the way it did. So, embrace those uncomfortable challenges and find the silver lining—you are incredibly powerful and there is no doubt that you will succeed!

If you have enjoyed reading this book, please leave a review.

PRINTABLE RESOURCES

Scan the QR code or use the link to download your
Goal and Weekly Productivity Planner to keep track of your
goals and progress.

https://bit.ly/3s4drmR

REFERENCES

Alberts, L. (2015, June 5). *Failure: Why it's actually good for your young athlete.* www.nays.org. https://www.nays.org/sklive/for-parents/failure-why-it-s-actually-good-for-your-young-athlete/

Anne, M. (2013, May 12). *The types of sacrifices athletes make.* Healthfully. https://healthfully.com/1002450-types-sacrifices-athletes-make.html

Astramskas, D. (2015, September 23). *Steph Curry reads an old negative scouting report in an inspirational ad.* Ballislife.com. https://ballislife.com/steph-curry-reads-an-old-negative-scouting-report-in-new-inspirational-ad/

Author, A. T. (2018, April 13). *Hard work beats talent when talent doesn't work hard for success.* Align Thoughts. https://alignthoughts.com/talent-or-hard-work/

AZQuotes. (n.d.). *Robbie Lawler quote.* A-Z Quotes. https://www.azquotes.com/quote/1065137

Baker, T. (2019, February 11). *What can we learn from the world's greatest sporting team?* www.linkedin.com. https://www.linkedin.com/pulse/what-can-we-learn-from-worlds-greatest-sporting-team-dr-tim-baker/

Bastie, F. (2017, July 19). *Recruiting column: How to deal with rejection in the college recruiting process.* USA Today High School Sports. https://usatodayhss.com/2017/recruiting-column-how-to-deal-with-rejection-in-the-college-recruiting-process

Biography.com Editors. (2017, April 28). *Babe Ruth. Biography.* https://www.biography.com/athlete/babe-ruth

Brodie, M. (2013, May 24). *Perfectionism and burnout.* Believe Perform. https://believeperform.com/perfectionism-and-burnout/#:~:text=Perfectionists%20are%20known%20for%20setting

Brown, L. (2020, December 21). *15 ways to speak your dreams into existence (with the Law of Attraction).* Nomadrs. https://nomadrs.com/speak-your-dreams-into-existence/

Clear, J. (2018). *James Clear.* James Clear. https://jamesclear.com/atomic-habits

Cohn, P. (2018, September 4). *How athletes can balance sports and life.* www.peaksports.com. https://www.peaksports.com/sports-psychology-blog/are-you-a-24-7-athlete-be-a-balanced-athlete/

Cohn, P. J., & Bekker, A. (n.d.). *Avoiding mental sabotage part 7: How to be dynamic instead of perfect.* www.trainingpeaks.com. https://www.trainingpeaks.com/blog/avoiding-mental-toughness-part-7-how-to-be-dynamic-instead-of-perfect/

Crowley, T. (n.d.). *6 Components to a successful training plan.* www.trainingpeaks.com. https://www.trainingpeaks.com/blog/6-components-to-a-successful-training-plan/

Fearless Motivation. (2017, September 13). *15 Of the best motivational quotes by great athletes on struggle and success.* Fearless Motivation. https://www.fearlessmotivation.com/2017/09/13/motivational-quotes-by-athletes/#:~:text=%E2%80%93%20Matt%20Biondi

Flynn, N. (2016, June 13). *What Muhammad Ali can teach us about belief systems and business.* www.linkedin.com. https://www.linkedin.com/pulse/what-muhammad-ali-can-teach-us-belief-systems-niamh-flynn-mba/

Fully Equipped Athlete. (2010, December). *The ultimate guide to game day routines for athletes.* Major League Mindset. https://fullyequippedathlete.com/blog/the-ultimate-guide-to-game-day-routines-for-athletes

Future Learn. (2021, July 21). *How to train like an athlete | Simple steps for exercising efficiently.* Future Learn. https://www.futurelearn.com/info/blog/how-to-train-like-athlete-tips

Gervais, M. (2020, March 20). *Disrupt your own narrative. Harvard Business Review.* https://hbr.org/2020/03/disrupt-your-own-narrative

Gill, G. (2017, April 16). *Building self-confidence in sport.* Believe Perform. https://believeperform.com/building-self-confidence-in-sport/

Goldberg, C. (2020, September 1). *The only 7 things you can really control in life.* Greatist. https://greatist.com/grow/what-you-can-control-for-happiness-success

Good Reads. (n.d.). *Kobe Bryant quotes* (Author of The Mamba Mentality). Www.goodreads.com. https://www.goodreads.com/author/quotes/5863606.Kobe_Bryant

Good Reads. (2019). *A quote by Albert Einstein.* Goodreads.com. https://www.goodreads.com/quotes/115696-genius-is-1-talent-and-99-percent-hard-work

Gupta, G. (2020, October 15). *The elite mentality of Cristiano Ronaldo.* www.theturffootball.com. https://www.theturffootball.com/articles/the-elite-mentality-of-cristiano-ronaldo/

Harper, B. (2019, August 15). *Baseball pro tips: Work ethic with Bryce Harper. Pro Tips by Dick's Sporting Goods.* https://protips.dickssportinggoods.com/sports-and-activities/baseball/baseball-pro-tips-work-ethic-with-bryce-harper

Harris-Fry, N. (2021, October 29). *Six ways you can train like a professional athlete.* Coach. https://www.coachmag.co.uk/fitness/8208/six-ways-you-can-train-like-a-professional-athlete

How beliefs are formed and how to change them. (2018). Skilledatlife.com. http://www.skilledatlife.com/how-beliefs-are-formed-and-how-to-change-them/

IResearchNet. (2016, October 20). *Goal setting in sports.* IResearchNet. http://psychology.iresearchnet.com/sports-psychology/psychological-skills/goal-setting-in-sports/

Janssen, J. (n.d.). *What kind of culture do you have? Discover the 8 kinds of culture.* Www.janssensportsleadership.com. https://www.janssensportsleadership.com/resources/janssen-blog/what-kind-of-culture-do-you-have-discover-the-7-kinds-of-cultures/

Jennifer. (2019, December 12). *3 Important lessons on finding balance in life.* Simply Fiercely. https://www.simplyfiercely.com/finding-balance/

Jussim, M. (2016, May 4). *11 Sports stars who went from fat to fit.* Men's Journal. https://www.mensjournal.com/sports/11-sports-stars-who-went-fat-fit/

Kaplan, E. (2017, December 26). *How to rewire your brain for massive success, according to neuroscience.* Thrive Global. https://medium.com/thrive-global/how-to-rewire-your-brain-for-massive-success-according-to-neuroscience-f051a30395d1

Kidadl Team. (2021, November 23). *70 Motivational Serena Williams quotes to inspire you.* Kidadl.com. https://kidadl.com/articles/motivational-serena-williams-quotes-to-inspire-you

Kinsley, D. (n.d.). Neuroplasticity: *This is how to rewire your brain for success.* Blog.myneurogym.com. https://blog.myneurogym.com/neuroplasticity-train-your-brain-for-success

Kuik, R. (2019, May 14). *Mental health and athletes.* Athletes for Hope. https://www.athletesforhope.org/2019/05/mental-health-and-athletes/

Lee. (2021). *5 Ways to create high performance habits.* The Athlete Tribe. https://www.theathletetribe.com/5-ways-to-create-high-performance-habits/

Liles, M. (2021, January 7). *150 Good attitude quotes that'll help you get into a happier mindset.* Parade: Entertainment, Recipes, Health, Life, Holidays. https://parade.com/1145640/marynliles/attitude-quotes/

Mens Health Staff. (2021, May 1). *This is what professional athletes are sacrificing in life.* Men's Health Magazine Australia. https://www.menshealth.com.au/do-you-have-what-it-takes-to-be-a-pro-sportsman/

Monsma, E. V. (2018). *Principles of effective goal setting.* Appliedsportpsych.org. https://appliedsportpsych.org/resources/resources-for-athletes/principles-of-effective-goal-setting/

Montford, C. (2020, January 28). *What Mamba Mentality actually means, according to Kobe Bryant.* Showbiz Cheat Sheet; Showbiz Cheat Sheet. https://www.cheatsheet.com/entertainment/what-mamba-mentality-actually-means-according-to-kobe-bryant.html/

Nikolov, C. (2019, December 2). *Top 24 most motivating Cristiano Ronaldo quotes.* Motivation Grid. https://motivationgrid.com/top-24-motivating-cristiano-ronaldo-quotes/

O'Sullivan, J. (2021, September 21). *How to help your athletes build great habits and break the bad ones.* Changing the Game Project. https://changingthegameproject.com/how-to-help-your-athletes-build-great-habits-and-break-the-bad-ones/

Omar Itani. (2020, April 7). *Always choose to focus on what is within your control.* Omar Itani. https://www.omaritani.com/blog/learn-to-focus-on-what-is-within-your-control#:~:text=Within%20our%20control%20are%20our

Oppong, T. (2020, February 15). *The iceberg illusion: The hidden logic of success.* Ladders. https://www.theladders.com/career-advice/the-iceberg-illusion-the-hidden-logic-of-success

Paton, C. (2016, May 27). *"If you don't know where you are going, any road will take you there."* News24. https://www.news24.com/News24/if-you-dont-know-where-you-are-going-any-road-will-take-you-there-20160527

Polacek, S. (2016, May 25). *Eddie Lacy comments on weight loss, workout regimen and more.* Bleacher Report. https://bleacherreport.com/articles/2642212-eddie-lacy-comments-on-weight-loss-workout-regimen-and-more

Prince, C. (2017, April 21). *Scheduling your busy life.* Cary Prince Organizing. https://caryprinceorganizing.com/scheduling-busy-life/

Randall, O. (2021, March 19). *What is team culture?* Tribe365®. https://tribe365.co/what-is-team-culture/#:~:text=The%20definition%20of%20Team%20Culture

Ravindra. (2019, May 15). *Top 3 elements of work ethic.* Encore Sky Blog. https://encoresky.com/blog/top-3-elements-of-work-ethic/

Rizvi, A. (2012, September 10). *The fall and rise of maturing Serena Williams.* The National. https://www.thenationalnews.com/sport/the-fall-and-rise-of-maturing-serena-williams-1.632294/

Robinson, S. (2016, March 23). *Creating a sport support system that delivers.* www.nays.org. https://www.nays.org/sklive/for-coaches/creating-a-sport-support-system-that-delivers/

RSNG Team. (2020). *Ronaldo reveals the mindset and resilience needed to make it to the top.* Www.rsng.com. https://www.rsng.com/categories/movement-fuel/articles/ronaldo-reveals-the-mindset-and-resilience-needed-to-make-it-to-the-top

Sagdullaev, A. (2017, September 4). *How to handle success: 5 Important things to do after you succeed.* Medium. https://medium.com/@asagdullaev/how-to-handle-success-5-important-things-to-do-after-you-succeed-708c33d72876

Saviuc, L. D. (2015, January 8). *50 Quotes that will change the way you think.* Purpose Fairy. https://www.purposefairy.com/75123/50-quotes-that-will-change-the-way-you-think/

Seale, Q. (2000). *100 Most inspirational sports quotes of all time.* Keepinspiring.me. https://www.keepinspiring.me/100-most-inspirational-sports-quotes-of-all-time/

Smith, M. D. (2016, January 18). *Mike McCarthy tells Eddie Lacy to shape up or ship out. ProFootballTalk.* https://profootballtalk.nbcsports.com/2016/01/18/mike-mccarthy-tells-eddie-lacy-to-shape-up-or-ship-out/

Sniechowski, J. (2013, August 26). *Your reputation is not within your control: So what can you do?* www.linkedin.com. https://www.linkedin.com/pulse/20130826063808-85816712-your-reputation-is-not-within-your-control-so-what-can-you-do/

Sporting Bounce. (2021, February 18). *Experiencing and overcoming the pain of rejection in sport. Sporting Bounce.* https://www.sportingbounce.com/blog/experiencing-and-overcoming-the-pain-of-rejection-in-sport

Sprongo. (2018, December 6). *How setting goals can benefit athlete performance.* Sprongo. https://blog.sprongo.com/setting-goals-athlete-performance/

Stankovich, C. (2018, November 27). *Examining how confidence, anxiety, and fear impact athletic performance.* Dr. Stankovich. https://drstankovich.com/examining-how-confidence-anxiety-and-fear-impact-athletic-performance/

Stibel, J. (2017, August 29). *Michael Jordan: A profile in failure.* CSQ. https://csq.com/2017/08/michael-jordan-profile-failure/#.YfI6k0xBzIU

Surf Today. (n.d.). *The inspirational quotes by Bethany Hamilton.* Surfertoday. https://www.surfertoday.com/surfing/the-inspirational-quotes-by-bethany-hamilton

Swinburne. (2019, March 18). *The Iceberg Illusion.* Swinburne Online. https://www.swinburneonline.edu.au/blog/the-iceberg-illusion

Taylor, J. (2013, July 29). *Build a positive and high-performing sports team culture.* HuffPost; HuffPost. https://www.huffpost.com/entry/build-a-positive-and-high_b_3659341

Taylor, T. (2020, August 28). UFC: *How Robbie Lawler becomes ruthless in the Octagon.* Bleacher Report. https://bleacherreport.com/articles/2906558-ufc-how-robbie-lawler-becomes-ruthless-in-the-octagon

Tony Robbins. (2015, July 13). *Serena Williams training: On and off the court.* Tonyrobbins.com. https://www.tonyrobbins.com/career-business/ceo-lessons-from-serena-williams/

Turnbridge. (2020, April 29). *Tyson Fury's fight against mental health.* Turnbridge. https://www.turnbridge.com/news-events/latest-articles/tyson-fury-fight-against-drugs-and-mental-health/

University of Michigan. (n.d.). *Help yourself, help a friend - Athletes.* Caps. umich.edu. https://caps.umich.edu/article/help-yourself-help-friend-athletes

USA Today. (2016, June 3). *30 of Muhammad Ali's best quotes.* USA TODAY; USA TODAY. https://www.usatoday.com/story/sports/boxing/2016/06/03/muhammad-ali-best-quotes-boxing/85370850/

Western, D. (2019, January 29). *25 Motivational Stephen Curry quotes about success.* Wealthy Gorilla. https://wealthygorilla.com/16-motivational-stephen-curry-quotes-success/

White, M. G. (n.d.). *39 Sports quotes to get hyped and boost team spirit.* Examples.yourdictionary.com. https://examples.yourdictionary.com/39-sports-quotes-get-hyped-boost-team-spirit

Zipper, T. (2017, May 10). *15 Leadership lessons from the All Blacks.* Medium. https://medium.com/monday-motivator/15-leadership-lessons-from-the-all-blacks-e30d49ff8747

Made in the USA
Middletown, DE
08 February 2023

24376250R00070